"Beautifully written, biblically incisive, and culturally astute, *Together in Ministry* traces human flourishing in mutual male and female partnerships. Weaving wisdom from colleagues, researchers, and thought leaders, Rob Dixon exposes systemic barriers and offers a road map unleashing the power of mixed-gender leadership. *Together in Ministry* is balm to the church's soul."
Mimi Haddad, president of CBE International

"In this research-based and immensely practical book, Rob Dixon presents a model describing how men and women can develop flourishing partnerships in ministry. The book is winsome and transparent, laying out both benefits and barriers to mixed-gender ministry collaboration. Full of practical suggestions for successful partnerships, this book is a must-read for all Christians living out our calling as brothers and sisters in the body of Christ."
Leanne M. Dzubinski, associate professor at Cook School of Intercultural Studies, Biola University

"I'm convinced that the strategic vision Rob shares in this book will change the game for men and women, impacting every area of our lives. There is not a topic more important nor any better time than right now to read this book. The future is bright if we dare to change it together!"
Danielle Strickland, advocate and author of *Better Together: How Women and Men Can Heal the Divide and Work Together to Transform the Future*

"Deeply biblical and rigorously practical, *Together in Ministry* gives ministries the tools needed tools to benefit from God's design for healthy partnerships between women and men. The book challenged me to embrace the intentional practices Rob Dixon lays out and to foster the kind of culture that helps partnerships thrive."
Tom Lin, president, InterVarsity Christian Fellowship/USA

"The Christian ministry context is long overdue for healthy, practical models of women and men in ministry partnership. In *Together in Ministry*, Rob Dixon presents a timely and invaluable training model for forming mixed-gender partnerships that are both personally satisfying and missionally effective. Let this straightforward, honest, and pragmatic book be your guide for building flourishing relationships in your ministry!"
Lisa Rodriguez-Watson, national director, Missio Alliance

Together in

MINISTRY

Women and Men in Flourishing Partnerships

ROB DIXON

Foreword by RUTH HALEY BARTON

An imprint of InterVarsity Press
Downers Grove, Illinois

InterVarsity Press
P.O. Box 1400, Downers Grove, IL 60515-1426
ivpress.com
email@ivpress.com

InterVarsity Press® is the book-publishing division of InterVarsity Christian Fellowship/USA®, a movement of students and faculty active on campus at hundreds of universities, colleges, and schools of nursing in the United States of America, and a member movement of the International Fellowship of Evangelical Students. For information about local and regional activities, visit intervarsity.org.

Scripture quotations, unless otherwise noted, are from the New Revised Standard Version Bible, copyright © 1989 National Council of the Churches of Christ in the United States of America. Used by permission. All rights reserved worldwide.

While any stories in this book are true, some names and identifying information may have been changed to protect the privacy of individuals.

The publisher cannot verify the accuracy or functionality of website URLs used in this book beyond the date of publication.

Cover design and image composite: Cindy Kiple
Interior design: Daniel van Loon
Image: two people reaching up: © Imagezoo / Getty Images

ISBN 978-1-5140-0070-0 (print)
ISBN 978-1-5140-0071-7 (digital)

Printed in the United States of America ♾

Library of Congress Cataloging-in-Publication Data
Names: Dixon, Robert (Robert Ford), 1972- author.
Title: Together in ministry : women and men in flourishing partnerships / Robert Dixon.
Description: Downers Grove, IL : IVP Academic, [2021] | Includes bibliographical references and indexes.
Identifiers: LCCN 2021020561 (print) | LCCN 2021020562 (ebook) | ISBN 9781514000700 (paperback) | ISBN 9781514000717 (ebook)
Subjects: LCSH: Group ministry. | Women in church work. | Men in church work. | Church personnel management. | Man-woman relationships—Religious aspects—Christianity.
Classification: LCC BV675 .D59 2021 (print) | LCC BV675 (ebook) | DDC 253/.7—dc23
LC record available at https://lccn.loc.gov/2021020561
LC ebook record available at https://lccn.loc.gov/2021020562

| P | 25 | 24 | 23 | 22 | 21 | 20 | 19 | 18 | 17 | 16 | 15 | 14 | 13 | 12 | 11 | 10 | 9 | 8 | 7 | 6 | 5 | 4 | 3 | 2 | 1 |
| Y | 38 | 37 | 36 | 35 | 34 | 33 | 32 | 31 | 30 | 29 | 28 | 27 | 26 | 25 | 24 | 23 | 22 | 21 | 21 |

To Amy, my forever partner in life and ministry

CONTENTS

Foreword by Ruth Haley Barton   *ix*

Acknowledgments   *xiii*

Introduction: God's Intent for Flourishing Partnerships   *1*

1 The Together in Ministry Model   *15*

PART 1—INNER LIFE | 27

2 Authentic Learner's Posture   *29*

3 Shared Theological Conviction of Gender Equality   *40*

4 Awareness of Gender Brokenness   *52*

PART 2—COMMUNITY CULTURE | 63

5 Vision for Freely Shared Power   *65*

6 Differences for the Sake of Mission   *78*

7 Value for Holistic Friendships   *88*

8 Corporate Sensitivity to Adverse Gender Dynamics   *98*

PART 3—INTENTIONAL PRACTICES | 111

9 Abundant Communication   *113*

10 Contextualized Boundaries   *125*

11 Public Affirmation and Modeling   *137*

Conclusion: Together in Ministry   *147*

General Index   *153*

Scripture Index   *155*

FOREWORD

IN 1998 I PUBLISHED A BOOK called *Equal to the Task: Men and Women in Partnership at Work, at Church, and at Home.* It did not sell particularly well, perhaps because it was ahead of its time. Then in 2019 my editor at InterVarsity Press invited me to consider revising it and bringing it out again in response to the #MeToo and #ChurchToo movements, which were relentlessly exposing dark patterns of sexual misconduct, harassment, and discrimination against women both inside and outside the church. I agreed to do this revision, and I tried— I really did. But eventually I had to admit that I just wasn't up to the task of confronting, once again, these disturbing age-old patterns that have hurt women and men for so long. I had to acknowledge my disappointment and disillusionment that we had made so little progress on these things and, in fact, seemed to be going backward. But now I know the deeper reason why I did not take on this piece of work—and that is because Rob Dixon was supposed to do it!

The book you hold in your hand is the book I would have *wanted* to write had God led me to do it, but in reading his manuscript I am convinced that Rob is the God-ordained person to bring fresh perspectives on God's vision for women and men as equal partners in ministry and to help us walk it out. While honoring and referencing so much of the good work that has gone before, Rob's message is winsome and well-researched, biblically and historically grounded, full of practical guidance and lessons learned from real-life experiences. Yes, it addresses the necessity of equality and equity among women and men, but it goes far beyond that to point toward the greater goal of human flourishing and missional effectiveness in the lives of both men and women as they work together. His Together in Ministry model provides just the practical help we need to fully understand what is required and get after it.

My gratitude for Rob's investment in researching and writing this book is quite personal as well. As I considered the possibility of rewriting *Equal to the Task,* I realized part of my resistance was my hope that twenty years later such a book would no longer be needed—that we would have gotten beyond it and on to other things.

But then this happened: I was invited to speak at a national gathering by a senior leader in the organization. This man had read pretty much everything I had written on spiritual formation and transforming leadership and, in fact, was using much of it for leadership development throughout their organization. This was, of course, nice to hear, and having me come and address their conference seemed like a God-guided next step. He and his wife even traveled from out of state to come to my office so we could meet in person and discern together what my contribution might be. All good.

The event finally came, and I gave my first message. Following the first presentation I needed to have a brief meeting with the emcee to go over details for the next session along with a brief conversation with the senior leader to touch base on the content for my final message. Four of us—emcee, senior leader, an assistant, and myself—sat down together in a room right off a main hallway to work out the final details. Since the room where we were meeting held all the supplies and equipment for the event, there was the happy hustle and bustle of people entering and exiting, while my own associate was out in the hallway selling books.

We began by making decisions about the schedule, and then the emcee and the assistant got up to leave and carry on with their responsibilities. But as they were departing the room, to my surprise the senior leader said to them, "You can't both leave!" It took me a minute to understand what was going on, and he must have seen the look of incomprehension cross my face because he turned to me and said, "Oh, it's not about you. It's just that I've promised my wife I would never be alone with another woman." At this point his assistant turned around and came back to the table where we were working and sat down in the corner, trying to make herself scarce while (I guess) watching over us to make sure nothing inappropriate happened.

For a moment I was knocked off my game because now, rather than being present to the decisions we were making regarding the good and important ministry we were there to do, a feeling of awkwardness had descended. Even though I knew in my head that this had nothing to do with me specifically (except for the unavoidable fact that I was female), I was now managing real discomfort and vague feelings of shame about being a woman *and* being man and woman trying to do ministry together. I felt angry and disappointed that he had introduced such an awkward and demeaning dynamic into our work together, and all sorts of non-ministry-related thoughts were now running through my head: "Does he not trust me? Does he not trust himself? Does he not trust his people and what they might think?"

I was also embarrassed for his wife—whom I never would have perceived as being so insecure she would have needed him to make that kind of commitment. When we gathered for dinner, I was less comfortable with her and less comfortable with myself—aware that somehow I was viewed as not being quite safe. Knowing her husband would never have treated a male colleague this way, I now had to hold this painful awareness that being a woman put me in a slightly different category than the men this leader worked with. Rather than enjoying the experience of doing really good ministry in the context of a solid collegial relationship, it all felt just plain yucky.

I recovered myself quickly enough and soldiered on, but that incident changed everything. As I stood to speak and bring my part of the gathering to its conclusion, I struggled to focus on the ministry at hand while my mind continued to process what had taken place. In some ways I was still in shock that it had happened at all, and I kept thinking, "This is *not* what being brothers and sisters in Christ looks like or feels like!" This experience is really all I remember now about the entire event.

I share this very personal experience to illustrate the sad reality that a book like Rob's *Together in Ministry* is still needed. And while I would like to be able to say the church has been helpful regarding the pain and questions men and women experience in relation to each other, what happened to me that day reminded me that the church itself and individual Christians often contribute to the problem rather than help to solve it. We swing wildly between well-known Christian men who distinguish their Christian faith and practice by the fact that they do not dine alone or meet alone with women other than their spouses, while at the same time stories of sexual scandal and the abuse of power within Christian churches and ministries keep coming in waves.

Fortunately, Rob does not shy away from these and many other relevant issues in our quest for healthy relationships between women and men in ministry. His thesis—that a return to the Genesis picture of flourishing in mixed-gender partnerships is both necessary and possible—reminds us that Christians *could* come to be known for something much more life-giving than these wild extremes. As Rob states so compellingly, "God's creation intent for the full and equal partnership of women and men, affirmed so often in the Scriptures in both theology and practice, should be the goal that we strive for in our churches and organizations." He believes, as I do, that full and equal partnership between men and women is a biblically endorsed way for both genders to flourish *and* to accomplish God's kingdom purposes in the sex-crazed, power-abusing, one-up-one-down world we live in. He writes, "We must not rest until we have embodied God's Genesis vision for mixed-gender ministry partnerships," and I could not agree more.

That is why I am commending this book—its theological vision, its practical model, its penetrating wisdom and thought-provoking questions—for your prayerful consideration. Read it and weep, pray, talk, and change, because if you do, God's kingdom vision for women and men will come and God's will *will* be done—on earth as it is in heaven.

ACKNOWLEDGMENTS

THIS IS A BOOK ABOUT MINISTRY PARTNERSHIP, and so it is fitting to acknowledge the many partners who have helped me in the process of putting these words onto paper.

First, it has been my joy to serve alongside a number of amazing women in the context of our work with InterVarsity. Many have stories in this book, but not all. And while I won't name everyone for the sake of space, know that *Together in Ministry* would not be possible without you. My name appears on the cover of this book, but the many women I've worked alongside over the years are its coauthors.

Next, I owe a debt to everyone involved in my doctoral journey. Thanks to the sixty-three current and former InterVarsity staff who shared their experiences with me. You produced the raw material that resulted in this model. I had the joy of studying alongside a group of peers through the research process; thanks, all, for your support and encouragement. And I am grateful to Dr. Betsy Glanville and Dr. Susan Maros for guiding me through the doctorate journey. As a two-time alumnus and now as adjunct faculty, I am proud to be a part of a community of scholars and practitioners in the Fuller Seminary ecosystem.

Third, I want to acknowledge some individuals and organizations that have opened doors for me to field-test this model "in the wild." Thanks to Rev. Liz Testa, Lesley Mazzotta, Lorraine Parker, and Rev. April Fiet from the Reformed Church in America. It is an honor to partner with you in building God's church together! Thanks to Wendy Wilson, Dr. Leanne Dzubinksi and the folks at Missio Nexus for the opportunity to introduce my model to hundreds of leaders and organizations. The good people at Christians for Biblical Equality, especially Dr. Mimi Haddad, have been wonderful advocates for me, hosting the first-ever public presentation of the Together in Ministry model.

And a big thanks to InterVarsity. When I started my doctoral program, I did so with the knowledge that at the end of the process I would hand InterVarsity my dissertation and then hope that it would be welcomed. It has been. Thanks to many, and in particular to Greg Jao, Janet Balajthy, Tom Allen, Alec Hill, and Anne Hong, for your support and advocacy.

Fourth, thank you to those who partnered with me in the process of writing the book. Garrett Girard, Matt Meyer, Sarah Cowen Johnson, Destiny Echols, Jon Carrillo, and Melodie Marske were the first readers, offering helpful feedback on my initial draft. The folks at IVP Academic have been wonderful to partner with; thanks in particular to Jon Boyd and Rebecca Carhart. And then there are the #bookdoulas, a group of friends that faithfully prayed, sympathized, encouraged, and even harangued during the fourteen months (and counting!) this book has been in process. Thanks to Layla Van Gerpen, Matt Meyer, Nicole Kyker, and Todd Riddiough for helping to birth this book.

Finally, I'm grateful for friends and family. Thanks to Bob and Kendra Green for generously providing the funding for my doctoral project. You were the true early adopters! I am always grateful to the Dixons and Sextons for your support, and the biggest of shout-outs goes to my wife, Amy, and our kids: Josh, Lucy, Gracie, and Lily. Thanks for cheering me on and for caring for me during the ups and downs of the writing process. I'm proud to say that with the publishing of *Together in Ministry*, Dad is now just three books behind Mom!

May this book and the ideas within catalyze a new way of thinking about and expressing mixed-gender ministry partnerships in our faith communities, and may God's mission advance in greater measure because of it!

INTRODUCTION

IN A WAY, I HAVE BEEN WORKING on this book for the last twenty-seven years. Though I grew up in a church that modeled, however imperfectly, ministry partnerships between women and men, I didn't personally experience the reality of mixed-gender ministry partnerships until my first student leadership assignment with InterVarsity Christian Fellowship.

During my junior year in college, I intentionally moved back into one of the dorms on our campus for the purpose of facilitating a small group Bible study for first-year students. I was excited to try out leadership, but I was also nervous, mostly because I had never led a Bible study before. Thankfully, I got paired up with my friend Andy, and together we were joined by an InterVarsity staff worker named Úna. The idea was that Úna would mentor and develop Andy and me as leaders as we worked together to care for students in the dorm.

About three months into the endeavor, one of our small group members walked down the hall and into my dorm room. Sitting on my couch, he started our conversation by telling me how much he loved our small group, which was music to my anxious ears. From there, however, the conversation took a turn because this student also had a particular rebuke in mind.

To be specific, he told me that we were making a mistake by having Úna lead the actual Bible study portion of our meetings. I immediately pushed back, noting that Úna was the professional minister and that Andy and I were learning as we went along. Surely if this student wanted to experience quality Bible study, he should want Úna's skilled leadership! In response, he opened his Bible, and began to quote from 1 Timothy 2:12, the text where Paul commands silence from women in the Ephesian congregation. Not only was that the first time that I had encountered that particular passage, it was also the first time that anyone had questioned me regarding the appropriateness of the full and equal partnership of women and men in the work of ministry. That experience triggered an intensive season of study and contemplation, a season that has never really ended for me.

Much has happened in the twenty-seven years since this experience. I have explored both the theology and practice of mixed-gender ministry partnerships, and in this book you will find stories that illustrate both my victories and failures. Over time, my interest in this topic led me to offer teaching and training on mixed-gender ministry partnerships as I traveled to speak at various InterVarsity fellowships in my region.

Eventually, my casual interest took a more formal turn when I enrolled in the Doctor of Intercultural Studies program at Fuller Theological Seminary, with a project focused on women and men in ministry partnerships. This book is the fruit of that study. In *Together in Ministry*, I aspire to blend twenty-seven years of ministry experience and exploration with four years of focused doctoral research to lay out a model for flourishing mixed-gender ministry partnerships.

FOUNDATIONS IN GENESIS

Before introducing my research model, I want to anchor this work in the context of theology and church history.[1] Indeed, this book rests on the premise that women and men are designed to partner together in the work of fulfilling God's mission on earth.[2] The whole of Scripture testifies to this truth, but this principle gets its earliest and most profound articulation in the first chapter of Genesis.

Untainted by the toxic effects of human sin, the scenes described in the first chapter of Genesis capture God's creation intent for the full and equal partnership of women and men in ministry. Specifically, this concept is affirmed in Genesis 1 by the principles that both genders are equally vested with the image of God and that they are jointly called to steward the created world.

In Genesis 1:27, we learn that both women and men bear the image of God. There is no evidence in the text that one gender is blessed with more of the divine image than the other. Instead, both genders embody God's image, and,

---

[1]Though significant, this theological survey will be necessarily brief. For a fuller treatment of a theology that endorses the full partnership of women and men in ministry, see my curated recommendations at the end of chap. 3.
[2]My rhetorical choice is to use the phrasing "women and men" throughout this book as a way to balance out the more common phrasing of "men and women."

in part, this is the basis for the ministry partnerships that they are invited to enjoy with one another. "Both [woman and man] are made in the one image. God's image is seen in them, not in him or her. Inherent in the image, then, is the idea that we are made for relationships, that we are only truly human when we are beings-in-fellowship and will only become complete persons through others."[3]

In the same way that women and men are equal in essence, they are likewise equal in role. Genesis 1:28 reads, "God blessed them, and God said to them, 'Be fruitful and multiply, and fill the earth and subdue it; and have dominion over the fish of the sea and over the birds of the air and over every living thing that moves upon the earth.'" With this mandate, the first humans are tasked with stewarding the earth, and significantly, they are given the command together. In her book *Women Leaders and the Church*, Linda Belleville writes, "There is also equality in the social realm. Both male and female are commanded to exercise dominion over creation . . . there is no division or distinction of the roles here. The woman is given the same task and level of responsibility as the man."[4]

Despite the picture of equality articulated in Genesis, some commentators do indeed read hierarchy into the creation account. In Genesis 2:18, the first woman is referred to as a "helper" to the first man, a description that seems to connote lesser authority or status. The problem with this interpretation is that the Hebrew word for "helper" is *ezer*, which does not imply subservience. In fact, almost every other time the word *ezer* is used in the Old Testament, it is used to describe God as a "helper" to the nation of Israel. For instance, in Psalm 54:3-4, David writes,

> For the insolent have risen against me,
>> the ruthless seek my life;
>> they do not set God before them.
> But surely, God is my helper;
>> the Lord is the upholder of my life.

In texts such as Psalm 54, the *ezer* God is portrayed as Israel's rescuer and protector. Reflecting on the use of *ezer* in Genesis 2, Carolyn Custis James

---

[3]Derek Tidball and Dianne Tidball, *The Message of Women*, The Bible Speaks Today (Downers Grove, IL: InterVarsity Press, 2010), 33. The marriage context would surely be included in this idea of becoming complete people through others, but the concept applies to mixed-gender friendships and ministry partnerships as well.

[4]Linda Belleville, *Women Leaders and the Church: Three Crucial Questions* (Grand Rapids, MI: Baker Academic, 2000), 100.

writes, "God created his daughters to be *ezer*-warriors with our brothers. He deploys the *ezer* to break the man's aloneness by soldiering with him whole-heartedly and at full strength for God's gracious kingdom. The man needs everything she brings to their global mission."[5]

Combining the reality that women and men jointly share the image of God with their corporate call to steward the created world, we are able to discern God's creation intent for the flourishing of women and men in full and equal partnership. Put simply, mixed-gender ministry partnerships represent God's original plan for fulfilling God's mission on earth.[6]

A DISTORTION OF GOD'S INTENT

Tragically, the world as God intended only lasts two chapters before the arrival of human sin. Genesis 3 tells the story of humanity's fall into sin, where the mutual partnership on display in the creation account comes to an abrupt and painful end. The fall represents a fundamental distortion of God's creative intent, as for the first time a power dynamic is introduced between the genders. Speaking to the first woman in Genesis 3:16, God says,

> I will greatly increase your pangs in childbearing;
>   in pain you shall bring forth children,
> yet your desire shall be for your husband,
>   and he shall rule over you.

It is important to state that in the fall of humanity, God's creation intent for equality does not change; instead, the gendered hierarchy embedded in the curse is the tragic result of human sin. "Eve and Adam's disobedience throws the compass that had indicated the direction God intended human beings to follow out of alignment . . . the preponderance of tension, arrogance, hostility and even abuse between them is far from the Creator's plan."[7]

By and large, when it comes to women and men in partnership, the story of the Old Testament is the sad tale of this hierarchical curse coming to pass.

---

[5]Carolyn Custis James, *Half the Church: Recapturing God's Global Vision for Women* (Grand Rapids, MI: Zondervan, 2011), 113.
[6]God transcends humanity's conventions about gender, so *Together in Ministry* will avoid using gendered pronouns to describe God. As Judy L. Brown notes, "To attach gender significance to any of the references to God, and thus to conclude that God has sexuality in some sense, is to assign to God qualities belonging to humanity and the created order." See her "God, Gender and Biblical Metaphor," in *Discovering Biblical Equality: Complementarity Without Hierarchy*, ed. Ronald W. Pierce and Rebecca Merrill Groothuis (Downers Grove, IL: InterVarsity Press, 2004), 289.
[7]Tidball and Tidball, *The Message of Women*, 53.

Indeed, texts such as Hagar's abuse (Genesis 16:1-16; 21:9-21), the rape of Tamar (2 Samuel 13:1-22), and the gender-based depravity throughout the book of Judges constitute a collection of passages that Phyllis Trible has rightly labeled "texts of terror" for women.[8]

Even in the midst of the curse becoming reality, God's creation intent breaks through at points in the Old Testament narrative as God empowers women to further God's purposes. Rebecca Merrill Groothuis writes, "Deviations from this social norm did occur occasionally, when God would raise up female prophets who exercised spiritual and even civil leadership, thus indicating that women's normally subordinate role was a cultural matter and not a result of divine decree or of any inherent deficiency in femaleness per se."[9] Women such as Miriam, Rahab, Deborah, Ruth, and Esther leap off the Old Testament pages as noteworthy reminders of God's creation paradigm of equality and mutuality.[10]

Still, these examples are all too uncommon in the Old Testament narrative. As a result, the first-century world that Jesus was incarnated into was one marked by systematized misogyny. First-century women and men lived a fundamentally unequal existence, with little to no context for mixed-gender ministry partnerships.

JESUS AND THE GENESIS IDEAL

The New Testament incarnation of Jesus reaffirmed God's creation intent for equality and mutuality between women and men. This reality is demonstrated first in how Jesus engaged the women of his day, and second in the theological implications of his work on the cross.

For one thing, how Jesus treated women was a significant corrective to how men treated women in first-century Jewish culture. Mary J. Evans notes,

---

[8]Phyllis Trible, *Texts of Terror: Literary-Feminist Readings of Biblical Narratives* (Philadelphia: Fortress, 1984). Interestingly, there has recently been a move to rethink biblical narratives that have traditionally cast women in a negative light. For instance, Sandra Glahn aspires to "bring to light a number of women labeled 'bad girls' who deserve a fresh look," in *Vindicating the Vixens: Revisiting Sexualized, Vilified, and Marginalized Women of the Bible* (Grand Rapids, MI: Kregel Academic, 2017), 13.

[9]Rebecca Merrill Groothuis, *Good News for Women: A Biblical Picture of Gender Equality* (Grand Rapids, MI: Baker Books, 1996), 22.

[10]Miriam is referenced throughout the Pentateuch, most prominently in Exodus 15 and Numbers 12. Later the prophet Micah lauds Miriam's role in the salvation of Israel: "For I brought you up from the land of Egypt, and redeemed you from the house of slavery; and I sent before you Moses, Aaron, and Miriam" (Micah 6:4). Rahab's story is recounted in Joshua 2, and her actions are affirmed in Hebrews 11:31. For Deborah, see Judges 4–5 (see also chap. 6).

"[Jesus'] approach can accurately be described as revolutionary, and we must take care in assessing the impact of Jesus' approach from our 'post-revolution' standpoint, not to forget just how revolutionary it was."[11] Many passages make this point about Jesus, but three brief examples will suffice.

First, Jesus really saw women. In a historical period where women were habitually relegated to the social margins, Jesus made it a point to engage with women in meaningful ways. There is perhaps no greater example than the text in Mark 5:24-34, where Jesus pauses in the midst of an important errand to acknowledge and reward the faith of a woman who had touched his cloak in the hopes of becoming healed. Jesus' closing words, "Daughter, your faith has made you well; go in peace, and be healed of your disease," communicate not only his ability to heal but also his willingness to see and express affection for this marginalized woman.

Next, Jesus welcomed women into his circle of disciples. In the text of Luke 10:38-42, Jesus is at the home of Martha and her sister Mary. Given a house filled with people needing sustenance, Martha took on the traditional role for a woman in that day, preparing the meal in the kitchen. By contrast, Mary eschews this social convention, instead opting to sit at Jesus' feet, in the position of a disciple. Not only does Jesus refuse to shoo Mary away, he actually rebukes Martha for not joining her sister. "By means of this story, Luke expands the category of discipleship to include women as well as men."[12]

Finally, Jesus invited women into his work of sharing the gospel. Following his resurrection, Jesus reveals his messianic identity to Mary Magdalene (John 20:11-18). Their encounter in the garden ends with Jesus commissioning Mary to tell the rest of the disciples about his resurrection. Not only is Mary entrusted with Jesus' true identity, but in a time when the testimony of a woman was routinely and systematically discounted, Jesus commissions her into service as a gospel ambassador. Aída Besançon Spencer writes, "Jesus . . . broke convention by choosing women as the first witnesses to the greatest

---

[11]Mary J. Evans, *Woman in the Bible: An Overview of All the Crucial Passages on Women's Roles* (Downers Grove, IL: InterVarsity Press, 1983), 45. Writing more recently, Alice Mathews confirms Evans's summation when she labels Jesus "the divine counterpunch." "Among the hierarchies Jesus overturned was the gender-based hierarchy dominating life in Israel." *Gender Roles and the People of God: Rethinking What We Were Taught About Men and Women in the Church* (Grand Rapids, MI: Zondervan, 2017), 70.

[12]Greg W. Forbes and Scott D. Harrower, *Raised from Obscurity: A Narratival and Theological Study of the Characterization of Women in Luke-Acts* (Eugene, OR: Pickwick, 2015), 109. For more on the Martha and Mary story, see chap. 6.

event of all times, the resurrection, even though women were not considered valid witnesses in court."[13]

In his practice, then, Jesus routinely overturned the entrenched misogynistic social order, inviting women into various forms of connection and partnership. And yet Jesus' affirmation of God's creation intent extended beyond simply his actions. Jesus' work on the cross likewise reasserts and reaffirms the foundational gender equality expressed in the creation account, and the theological epicenter for this truth is Galatians 3:26-29, particularly verse 28:

> For in Christ Jesus you are all children of God through faith. As many of you as were baptized into Christ have clothed yourselves with Christ. There is no longer Jew or Greek, there is no longer slave or free, there is no longer male and female; for all of you are one in Christ Jesus. And if you belong to Christ, then you are Abraham's offspring, heirs according to the promise.

Some scholars interpret this text as having solely salvific implications, arguing that Paul's message is merely that God doesn't show partiality in who can be saved. For instance, S. Lewis Johnson Jr. concludes that "there is no reason to claim that Galatians 3:28 supports an egalitarianism of function in the church. It does plainly teach an egalitarianism of privilege in the covenantal union of believers in Christ. The Abrahamic promises, in their flowering by the Redeemer's saving work, belong universally to the family of God."[14]

While this reading of the text is certainly accurate, it is also insufficient. In Galatians 3:28, Paul means to emphasize the social implications of Jesus' work on the cross in addition to the salvific ones. Walter Hansen writes, "The new vertical relationship with God results in a new horizontal relationship with one another. All racial, economic and gender barriers and all other inequalities are removed in Christ. The equality and unity of all in Christ are not an addition, a tangent or an optional application of the gospel. They are part of the essence of the gospel."[15] In a world where women had next to no status, Paul's grand statement serves to reset the Genesis paradigm; in the work of Jesus on

---

[13]Aída Besançon Spencer, "Jesus' Treatment of Women in the Gospels," in *Discovering Biblical Equality: Complementarity Without Hierarchy*, ed. Ronald Pierce and Rebecca Merrill Groothuis (Downers Grove, IL: InterVarsity Press, 2004), 139. For more on Jesus' interaction with Mary in the garden in John 20, see chap. 9.

[14]S. Lewis Johnson Jr., "Role Distinctions in the Church: Galatians 3:28," in *Recovering Biblical Manhood and Womanhood: A Response to Evangelical Feminism*, ed. John Piper and Wayne Grudem (Wheaton, IL: Crossway, 2006), 164.

[15]G. Walter Hansen, *Galatians*, IVP New Testament Commentary Series (Downers Grove, IL: InterVarsity Press), 112.

the cross, women and men are restored to equal status, and God's vision for mixed-gender ministry partnership is reaffirmed.

THE FIRST CHURCH FOLLOWS JESUS' EXAMPLE

Following after the example of Jesus, the first church found ways for women and men to partner together in ministry. Time and again, the New Testament church follows God's blueprint for the full and equal partnership of women and men in ministry, even in a culture marked by rampant misogyny.

The apostle Paul, writer of Galatians 3:26-29, put his theology into practice, as his cohort was filled with women who served as ministry partners. Paul partnered with Phoebe, the deaconess of Cenchreae (Romans 16:1), who likely carried and exposited the letter to the church in Rome.[16] He also worked alongside Lydia, a woman whom many scholars consider the leader of the house church in Philippi (Acts 16:11-40). And Paul partnered with his relative Junia, a woman called "prominent among the apostles" (Romans 16:7).

The list of Paul's female partners could go on to include women such as Lois and Eunice (2 Timothy 1:5), Tryphaena and Tryphosa (Romans 16:12), Damaris (Acts 17:34), and Nympha (Colossians 4:15), among others. Indeed, the first church was full of prophetesses, deaconesses, and female teachers and apostles. Philip Payne writes, "For centuries, the apostle Paul has been castigated as a stone-faced misogynist with a particular dislike for women. Yet reading his letters reveals, instead, a man deeply invested in relationships with both men and women. He accepts women as ministry leaders and respects and honors women who labor for the Lord, not as his subordinates, but as his partners and equals."[17]

When Payne describes Paul's reputation in some circles as a "stone-faced misogynist," texts like 1 Timothy 2:11-12, referenced in the opening story of this chapter, come into focus. Over the years, there has been plenty of commentary about Paul's instructions to his protégé Timothy in that text, with many interpreting Paul's command for women to be silent as proof that he was in fact anti-women. To the contrary, there is compelling evidence that suggests that in 1 Timothy 2, Paul is instructing Timothy to deal with a situation particular to the Ephesian church, of which Timothy was the pastor. The

---

[16]For more on Phoebe, see chaps. 7 and 8.
[17]Philip B. Payne, *Man and Woman, One in Christ: An Exegetical and Theological Study of Paul's Letters* (Grand Rapids, MI: Zondervan, 2009), 61.

thinking is that women in the Ephesian church were in some way propagating false teaching, causing Paul to command his mentee to demand their silence until they could learn a more accurate reading of the Scriptures. Reflecting on this text, biblical scholar Craig Keener writes, "Given women's lack of training in the Scriptures, the heresy spreading in the Ephesian churches through ignorant teachers and the false teachers' exploitation of these women's lack of knowledge to spread their errors, Paul's prohibition here makes good sense. His short-range solution is that these women should not teach; his long-range solution is 'let them learn.'"[18] In this way, the text from 1 Timothy 2:11-12 harmonizes with Paul's theology and practice around gender equality.

Beyond the pages of the New Testament, there is an ever-growing wealth of evidence that the developing church likewise embraced the Genesis model of mixed-gender ministry partnership. For instance, Lynn Cohick and Amy Brown Hughes chronicle the stories of a number of women who held significant roles during the formation of the church between the second and fifth centuries. Included in this list is an ascetic named Thecla, so renowned that "men in the sixth century embraced an ascetic lifestyle based on her example."[19]

Further, we know that the list of martyrs is a mixed-gender list. As just one example, church historian Eusebius had this to say about Blandina, martyred in 177:

> Blandina was filled with such power that those who tortured her from morning to night grew exhausted and admitted that they were beaten, for they had nothing left to do to her. They were astounded that she was still alive, since her whole body was smashed and lacerated. . . . But the blessed woman, like a noble athlete, gained in strength while confessing the faith and found comfort in her sufferings by saying, 'I am a Christian, and nothing wicked happens among us.'"[20]

Lastly, in her book, *When Women Were Priests*, Karen Jo Torjeson writes, "The last thirty years of American scholarship have produced an amazing range

---

[18]Craig S. Keener, *The IVP Bible Background Commentary: New Testament* (Downers Grove, IL: InterVarsity Press, 1993), 611.

[19]Lynn H. Cohick and Amy Brown Hughes, *Christian Women in the Patristic World: Their Influence, Authority, and Legacy in the Second through Fifth Centuries* (Grand Rapids, MI: Baker Academic, 2017), xxix.

[20]Eusebius, *The Church History*, trans. Paul L. Maier (Grand Rapids, MI: Kregel Academic, 2007), 154. Blandina's endurance was notable, but she was indeed ultimately martyred. In her book *Feminine Threads*, Diana Lynn Severance chronicles Blandina's eventual passing: "Blandina was scourged, thrown to wild animals, and placed on a red-hot iron seat so that her flesh was burned. Finally, she was placed in a net and thrown before a bull." Diana Lynn Severance, *Feminine Threads: Women in the Tapestry of Christian History* (Scotland: Christian Focus, 2012), 40.

of evidence for women's roles as deacons, priests, presbyters, and even bishops in Christian churches from the first through the thirteenth century."[21] Even in a culture of rampant misogyny, the first church bravely strove to adhere to God's Genesis vision for full and equal mixed-gender ministry partnerships.

A History of Falling Short

Unfortunately, in the years following these promising initial steps, the church's lived experience has too often failed to align with the Genesis mandate for full and equal mixed-gender ministry partnerships. In good part, this downturn was provoked by a misogynistic theological strain that effectively relegated women to the margins of church life. Some two hundred years after the apostle Paul affirmed the Genesis vision for full mixed-gender partnerships in Galatians 3:28, early church leader Tertullian wrote to women, "And do you not know that you are (each) an Eve? The sentence of God on this sex of yours lives in this age: the guilt must of necessity live too. You are the devil's gateway; you are the unsealer of that (forbidden) tree: you are the first deserter of the divine law; you are she who persuaded him whom the devil was not valiant enough to attack. You destroyed so easily God's image, man. On account of your desert—that is, death—even the Son of God had to die."[22] In alignment with Tertullian's perspective on Eve, fourth-century theologian John Chrysostom noted that "the woman taught once, and ruined all. On this account, therefore [Paul] saith, let her not teach . . . for the sex is weak and fickle."[23]

Sadly, quotations like these represent just the beginning of this misogynistic theological thread. In *Summa Theologica*, Thomas Aquinas wrote, "As

---

[21]Karen Jo Torjesen, *When Women Were Priests: Women's Leadership in the Early Church & the Scandal of Their Subordination in the Rise of Christianity* (New York: HarperOne, 1993), 2.

[22]Tertullian, *On the Apparel of Women*, ed. Alexander Roberts and James Donaldson, trans. S. Thelwell, Ante-Nicene Fathers: The Writings of the Fathers Down to AD 325 (Peabody, MA: Hendrickson, 1995), 14.

[23]John Chrysostom, *Homily 9 on 2 Timothy*, ed. Philip Schaff, Nicene and Post-Nicene Fathers, vol. 13 (Peabody, MA: Hendrickson, 1995), 436. Though Chrysostom's odious view of women contributed to this theological problem for the church, it is worth noting that he also had some positive things to say, particularly about selected women in the Bible. For instance, reflecting on Junia's apostolic designation from Romans 16:7, Chrysostom writes, "And indeed to be apostles at all is a great thing. But to be even among these of note, just consider what great praise this is! But they were of note owing to their works, to their achievements. Oh! How great is the 'devotion' of this woman, that she should be even counted worthy of the appellation of apostle!" People can be complicated, and reconciling these two seemingly contradictory perspectives in Chrysostom's teaching is certainly a challenge. For more on Chrysostom and women, see Marg Mowczko, "Chrysostom on 5 Women Church Leaders in the NT," *Marg Mowczko* (blog), June 10, 2020, https://margmowczko.com/chrysostom-new-testament-women-leaders/.

regards the individual nature, woman is defective and misbegotten, for the active force in the male seed tends to the production of a perfect likeness in the masculine sex; while the production of woman comes from defect in the active force or from some material indisposition."[24] Similarly, Jean Calvin wrote, "Now Moses shews that the woman was created afterwards, in order that she might be a kind of appendage to the man; and that she was joined to the man on the express condition, that she should be at hand to render obedience to him."[25]

The impact of more than two thousand years of this aberrant and toxic strain of theology has been and continues to be profound. Because of this theology, misogyny has been encoded into the DNA of the church, and as a result God's Genesis vision has been largely obscured for two centuries of the church's existence.

Tragically, the edifice of today's church rests atop this foundation. For example, consider the reality that church leadership roles continue to largely be the domain of men. According to a recent study from the Barna Research Group, only 9 percent of senior pastor positions in American Protestant churches are currently occupied by women.[26] Though this represents a threefold increase from twenty-five years prior, it is still wildly out of balance. And while 79 percent of Americans express an openness to women serving as a pastor or priest, that is less true in evangelical churches, where only 39 percent are open to the idea of women serving in pastoral leadership roles. If today's church is to emulate the Genesis paradigm for flourishing mixed-gender ministry partnerships, we have plenty of work to do, both in changing hearts and minds as well as in addressing structural and systemic imbalances.

RETURNING TO THE GENESIS IDEAL

The thesis of this book is that a renewed embrace of the Genesis picture of flourishing mixed-gender ministry partnerships is both necessary and possible. God's creation intent for the full and equal partnership of women and men, affirmed so often in the Scriptures in both theology and practice,

---

[24]Aquinas, *Summa Theologica,* Question 92, reply to objection 1, trans. Fathers of the English Dominican Province (Westminster, MD: Christian Classics, 1981), 466.

[25]Jean Calvin, *Commentaries on the Epistles to Timothy, Titus, and Philemon,* trans. William Pringle (Grand Rapids, MI: Eerdmans, 1948), 69.

[26]Barna Research Group, "What Americans Think About Women in Power," March 8, 2017, www .barna.com/research/americans-think-women-power/.

should be the goal that we strive for in our churches and organizations. We must not rest until we have embodied God's Genesis vision for mixed-gender ministry partnerships.

Not only is a return to the Genesis ideal necessary, it is also possible. Churches and organizations can fulfill God's creation intent. To be sure, it will take intentionality and courage, but it is possible. And the model outlined in this book can help our communities, churches, and organizations get there.

Together in Ministry begins in chapter one with an overview of my research model for flourishing mixed-gender ministry partnerships. As individuals and communities build partnerships marked by the content of this model, they are more likely to see those partnerships become places of flourishing. Following this overview chapter, I will spend a full chapter profiling each of the ten attributes that constitute the Together in Ministry model. Since the attributes are intertwined, my recommendation is to read each one. Still, if readers are more interested in some over others, they can find what they are looking for in particular chapters.

In each chapter, I will explain an attribute of flourishing mixed-gender ministry partnerships, link that attribute to Scripture, provide an analysis of the benefits and barriers that can come with embracing and living out the attribute, and then offer ideas for how individuals and communities can embody the attribute in greater measure. I will close each chapter with processing questions designed to help readers envision what this attribute could look like lived out in their lives and ministries. After explaining each component of the model, I will close the book with a chapter discussing implications and application.

For some readers, the theological and historical presentation outlined in this introductory chapter will be easily received. For others, it may challenge deeply held assumptions. For both groups, my encouragement is to read on. In the end, my hope is that *Together in Ministry* will serve as a prophetic road map for individuals and communities as they discern ways to live out flourishing mixed-gender ministry partnerships in their contexts. May God grant us the courage to intentionally recapture the Genesis vision of the full and equal partnership of women and men in ministry!

PROCESSING QUESTIONS

  1. What work have you done with the Scriptures on the topic of women and men in ministry partnership? From this survey of Scripture and

church history, what was new for you? What challenged you? What would you like to explore further?

2. As you consider both church history and our current reality, where do you see roadblocks that prohibit women and men from serving together in full and equal partnerships? What would you need to get beyond those roadblocks, both personally and corporately?

3. As you begin this book, what questions do you have about women and men working together in ministry partnerships?

4. What are your hopes as you prepare to engage this topic more fully?

1

THE TOGETHER IN MINISTRY MODEL

THE FIRST AIM OF MY DOCTORAL RESEARCH was to determine the best combination of attributes that constitute flourishing mixed-gender ministry partnerships. Following that determination, my goal was to assemble those attributes into a model that individuals and communities could use to build such partnerships in greater measure. Before laying out the Together in Ministry model, some introductory definitions and background regarding the notion of *flourishing mixed-gender ministry partnerships* are in order.

MINISTRY PARTNERSHIPS

To begin with, my focus is the particular context of Christian *ministry. Ministry* includes any activity where the good news about Jesus is being proclaimed, either in word or deed. In my case, my research was conducted among individuals on staff with InterVarsity Christian Fellowship/USA. InterVarsity is a seventy-five-year-old evangelical campus ministry based in the United States whose stated purpose is "to establish and advance at colleges and universities witnessing communities of students and faculty who follow Jesus as Savior and Lord: growing in love for God, God's word, God's people of every ethnicity and culture, and God's purposes in the world." In InterVarsity's ministry, women and men partner together every day, in a variety of configurations.

My study began with InterVarsity, but since then I have noticed that my findings have relevance and applicability in other ministry contexts as well. As I have presented this content to a wide range of churches and organizations, including Wycliffe, Cru, Missio Nexus, and the Reformed Church in America, I have seen people helped by what I have discovered. It has been gratifying to watch the Together in Ministry model helpfully transcend organizational boundaries and denominational distinctives into a wide range of ministry contexts.

Next, in my research interviews and focus groups, I investigated many different forms of ministry *partnerships*. In some cases, partnerships were marked by an organizational power dynamic, with one of the partners serving as a supervisor to the other. In other cases, partners were peers, operating either as long-standing coworkers or in short-term arrangements. Some partners worked closely together and others over distance. This research is informed by a diversity of partnership arrangements, thus increasing its relevance to a variety of organizational contexts.

MIXED-GENDER

Next, by the term *mixed-gender*, I am specifically referring to ministry partnerships between women and men. The conversation around gender is alive right now in many spaces—including within some Christian churches and organizations—but during my research process, I opted to confine myself solely to ministry partnerships between women and men, and therefore *Together in Ministry* will be similarly restrained.[1] I will not, then, have anything specific to say about gender fluidity, transgenderism, or LGBTQ+ issues, though these topics are certainly worthy of further study.[2]

Instead, I have been curious about what makes ministry partnerships specifically between women and men work well, and *Together in Ministry* represents my answer to that question. No doubt each reader can bring to mind someone from the opposite gender with whom they work or serve in some sort of ministry context. In fact, it will be useful for readers to read this book with this person, or these people, in view. Better still, mixed-gender ministry partners can read this book together! In *Together in Ministry*, I aspire to equip individuals and communities to steward these partnerships well.

FLOURISHING

Finally, in *Together in Ministry* I will join with a growing chorus of writers and thinkers in using the term *flourishing* to capture the essence of what I hope these mixed-gender partnerships can become. The concept of flourishing is a popular

---

[1]When I began my research study in 2014, I used the term *inter-gender partnerships in mission*, but I realized that I would need further clarity going forward. By the time I was preparing my dissertation in the summer of 2017, I was using the term *male/female ministry partnerships*. More recently, I've landed on the more streamlined *mixed-gender ministry partnerships*.
[2]Likewise, *Together in Ministry* will stop short of a full-blown discussion about how social factors such as race and class intersect with gender in someone's lived experience. While reflection on the intersection of various factors deserves a full treatment, it is beyond the scope of my research process.

one in many Christian circles. For instance, in his book *Strong and Weak*, Andy Crouch defines flourishing as being "fully alive."[3] When something is fully alive, it is functioning as it was meant to function. Everything is working as intended, whether we're talking about a person, a relationship, or a system.

The Hebrew notion of shalom offers a biblical analog to how Crouch, myself, and others are using the term *flourishing*. When someone or something is experiencing shalom, it is truly flourishing and fully alive. In her book *The Very Good Gospel*, Lisa Sharon Harper captures the holistic nature of shalom:

> Shalom is what the Kingdom of God smells like. It's what the Kingdom looks like and what Jesus requires of the Kingdom's citizens. It's when everyone has enough. It's when families are healed. It's when shame is renounced and inner freedom is laid hold of. It's when human dignity, bestowed by the image of God in all humanity, is cultivated, protected, and served in families, faith communities, and schools and through public policy. Shalom is when the capacity to lead is recognized in every human being and when nations join together to protect the environment.[4]

What a vivid and compelling picture of shalom and, by extension, of human flourishing.

In the context of my research, mixed-gender ministry partnerships are flourishing when two things are true. First, ministry partners experience a profound sense of personal satisfaction. That is, the partnership is a blessing to each person involved. It is enjoyable, enriching, and life giving. More often than not, both partners go home at the end of the day grateful to be in partnership together.

Second, flourishing mixed-gender ministry partnerships accomplish something. They are not just personally satisfying; they are also missionally effective. In other words, the work produced is better specifically because of the partnership. Plenty of studies attest to the positive impact of diversity on an organization's bottom line, and flourishing partnerships experience that on a regular basis.[5]

---

[3] Andy Crouch, *Strong and Weak: Embracing a Life of Love, Risk and True Flourishing* (Downers Grove, IL: InterVarsity Press, 2016), 11.

[4] Lisa Sharon Harper, *The Very Good Gospel: How Everything Wrong Can Be Made Right* (New York: WaterBrook, 2016), 14.

[5] For more on this idea, see chap. 6, which engages the correlation between gender diversity and ministry growth and development.

These two characteristics—personal satisfaction and missional effectiveness—define what flourishing can look like in mixed-gender ministry partnerships.[6] When either of these two characteristics are absent or underdeveloped, partnerships won't be fully alive.

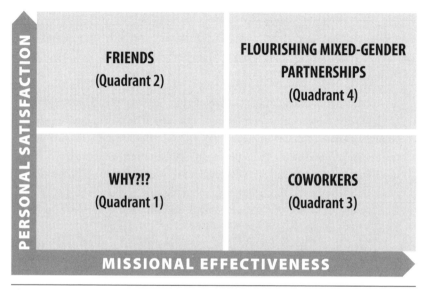

Figure 1.1. Personal satisfaction and missional effectiveness

Figure 1.1 further fills out this idea, using four quadrants to describe what happens as these two dimensions of flourishing increase or decrease. In quadrant one, both personal satisfaction and missional effectiveness are low, and one wonders why the partnership exists at all. After all, no one wants to be a part of a ministry partnership that is relationally dissatisfying and produces little fruit.

Quadrants two and three are better but still incomplete. In quadrant two, partnerships marked by high personal satisfaction but low missional effectiveness make for solid mixed-gender friendships, which are no small thing. As will be noted in chapter seven, life-giving mixed-gender friendships are important. Still, the lack of missional fruit limits such a partnership from being all that it could be in the ministry context.

---

[6]I am borrowing these two axes of flourishing mixed-gender ministry partnerships from Carol Becker's talismanic work *Becoming Colleagues: Women and Men Serving Together in Faith* (San Francisco, CA: Jossey-Bass, 2000): "Mixed-gender teams in which all the members say that their work is effective and mutually satisfying are the exception rather than the norm" (9).

In quadrant three, where missional effectiveness is high but personal satisfaction is low, lots of things get done but without accompanying personal fulfillment. As with the quadrant two example above, mixed-gender partnerships that expand the mission are still significant. And yet most work relationships marked by this reality will wear down over time. Even productive partnerships can wither without a robust interpersonal foundation.

Quadrant four, then, is the place of true flourishing, the quadrant where mixed-gender partnerships can be fully alive. It is the place of shalom. In quadrant four, personal satisfaction and missional effectiveness come together in a beautiful picture of flourishing mixed-gender ministry partnership.

As will become apparent throughout this book, I have been fortunate to personally experience the reality of flourishing mixed-gender partnerships. I know what quadrant four is like! For many years, I worked together in ministry with my friend Tina. Partnering together with Tina in ministry has been an interpersonal joy for us. Such is the nature of our friendship and working partnership that over the years we have regularly sought out opportunities to work together. On top of that, our partnership extends past the lines of work, as Tina is our family's official photographer, Tina's father served as our realtor, we trained for and ran a marathon together, and I officiated at Tina's wedding to her husband, Adam. In my ministry partnership with Tina, it has been a joy to experience a high degree of personal satisfaction.

At the same time, working together with Tina has repeatedly produced fruitful and effective ministry. Perhaps the best example of that is a seminar we lead that invites college students to explore the Bible's message of gender equality (see chap. 3). Our partnership is a true gift for our students in at least three ways. First, since Tina and I see the world through our distinctive lenses, the students benefit from our diverse perspectives. Second, serving in partnership permits students to choose to engage with the leader they connect with better, thus increasing our accessibility. Finally, our effective colaboring provides a real-time model that illustrates the very content we are studying.

By God's grace, my ministry partnership with Tina demonstrates the twin axes of flourishing mixed-gender ministry partnerships: personal satisfaction and ministry effectiveness. Next, I will provide an overview for how individuals and communities can build such partnerships in greater measure.

Ten Attributes of Flourishing Mixed-Gender Ministry Partnerships

During the course of my research, I engaged a diverse sample of more than sixty campus ministers working or formerly working with InterVarsity Christian Fellowship. Using the qualitative research methodologies of semi-structured interviews, focus groups, and participant observation, I sought answers to my primary research question: What collection of attributes compose flourishing mixed-gender ministry partnerships for my research participants?

After approximately two years of research, I gathered and coded the data, looking for common themes. Eventually, ten attributes emerged as critical for flourishing mixed-gender ministry partnerships. In other words, these ten characteristics constitute the raw material from which personally satisfying and missionally effective mixed-gender partnerships are formed. This book will devote a chapter to each attribute, but I will mention them in brief here.

First, mixed-gender ministry partnerships flourish when both members are committed to maintaining an authentic learner's posture. When people are eager and able to walk in one another's shoes, trust is formed and partnerships are more likely to flourish.

Second, a shared theological conviction that God honors the full and equal partnership of women and men marks flourishing partnerships. Ministry partners must be on the same page that full and equal partnerships between women and men are a biblically sanctioned way to accomplish God's kingdom purposes.

Third, when a person has a deepening awareness of their personal gender brokenness, they will be more equipped to form flourishing partnerships. Gender brokenness can take many forms, but when a person is aware of their shortcomings, they are able to take proactive steps to engage in mixed-gender ministry partnerships with greater wholeness.

Fourth, flourishing partnerships embody a vision for freely shared power. When partners are able to embrace and live out a countercultural model of shared power, there is more likely to be flourishing. Included in this attribute are concepts such as mutual advocacy, voluntary submission, and the paradigm that all voices are welcomed around the table.

Fifth, flourishing mixed-gender ministry partnerships are marked by a belief that embracing difference advances the mission. Whether or not differences adhere to the stereotypical picture of gender differences, in flourishing mixed-gender ministry partnerships people are free to lead in ways that are authentic to them. When differences are acknowledged and affirmed, they can be leveraged to advance the mission, often with exponential effects.

Sixth, flourishing mixed-gender ministry partnerships are simultaneously thriving friendships. Trust is formed as ministry partners share their whole lives with one another. While this attribute can be tricky, in part because it can challenge our notions of work/life balance, women and men are more likely to build flourishing partnerships when they are able to find a way to become both colleagues and friends.

Seventh, when teams and communities are able to cultivate a corporate sensitivity to adverse gender dynamics, flourishing partnerships can thrive. The social and organizational playing fields too often tilt in favor of men, and when communities have a radar for the subtle things that perpetuate that bias, they become able to mitigate those dynamics and mixed-gender ministry partnerships are empowered to flourish.

Eighth, abundant communication is central for flourishing partnerships. Consistent and vulnerable communication should saturate a partnership from beginning to end, including setting up the partnership, resolving conflict, and frequent debriefing. Simply put, if mixed-gender ministry partners cannot communicate effectively, their partnership will struggle to flourish.

Ninth, flourishing mixed-gender ministry partnerships are defined by contextualized interpersonal boundaries, tailored for each particular ministry partnership. Once they are clear on these contextualized boundaries, women and men can live out their partnerships with integrity and accountability.

Finally, flourishing mixed-gender ministry partnerships are more likely to become a reality when there is a public dimension to them. Indeed, when people see models of flourishing partnerships around them, they are inspired to create them themselves. In addition, verbally reinforcing the value is critical, as is intentionally pursuing diverse representation in a variety of ministry contexts.

Taken together, these ten attributes serve as the clay out of which flourishing mixed-gender ministry partnerships are formed. As individuals and communities pursue these attributes, my research shows that they will experience a higher degree of both personal satisfaction and missional effectiveness.

Three Domains of Flourishing

After establishing this tenfold roster of attributes, my next task was to form them into a viable training model. I began this process by grouping the ten attributes into three larger domains.

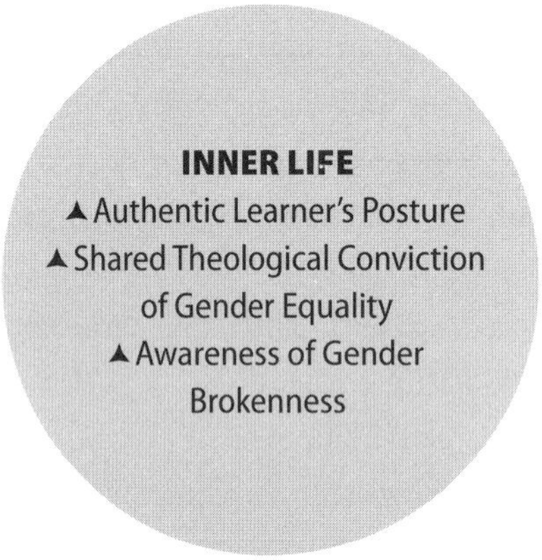

Because we bring who we are into the ministry partnerships we establish, the inner life domain captures who someone is or is in the process of becoming. This domain encompasses the attributes of an authentic learner's posture, a shared theological conviction of gender equality, and an awareness of gender brokenness (see fig. 1.2).

INNER LIFE
▲ Authentic Learner's Posture
▲ Shared Theological Conviction of Gender Equality
▲ Awareness of Gender Brokenness

Figure 1.2. The inner life domain

Next, the community culture in which a mixed-gender ministry partnership is situated will be critical in determining whether or not that partnership will be allowed to flourish. If the community or organizational culture endorses mixed-gender ministry partnerships, they have a greater possibility of flourishing. Unfortunately, the converse is also true. Attributes that populate the community culture domain include a vision for freely shared power, differences for the sake of mission, a value for holistic friendships, and a corporate sensitivity to adverse gender dynamics (see fig. 1.3).

COMMUNITY CULTURE
▲ Vision for Freely Shared Power
▲ Differences for the Sake of Mission
▲ Value for Holistic Friendships
▲ Corporate Sensitivity to Adverse Gender Dynamics

Figure 1.3. The community culture domain

Third, the intentional practices domain encompasses three tangible things that people and communities do in order to form flourishing mixed-gender ministry partnerships. Specifically, the attributes of abundant communication, contextualized boundaries, and public affirmation and modeling make up the intentional practices domain (see fig. 1.4).

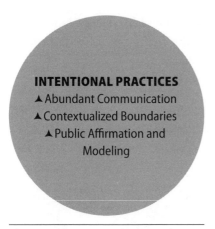

INTENTIONAL PRACTICES
▲ Abundant Communication
▲ Contextualized Boundaries
▲ Public Affirmation and
Modeling

Figure 1.4. The intentional practices domain

THE TOGETHER IN MINISTRY MODEL

After articulating the roster of ten attributes and grouping them into three larger domains, I determined that the best way to express the interconnectedness between the various elements was to use a Venn diagram. This enabled me to express two core principles regarding the model.

First, the middle of the diagram, where all three domains converge, is the sweet spot or target. This is the quadrant-four place of flourishing, where mixed-gender ministry partnerships are formed that are simultaneously personally satisfying and missionally effective. From my research, it became clear that each of the ten attributes contribute to flourishing partnerships, and the Venn diagram allowed me to represent that in a visual way.[7]

Second, the Venn diagram allowed me to imagine what would happen if one of the three domains is absent or significantly underdeveloped. For instance, if the inner life domain is removed, individuals and communities are left with a culture that endorses flourishing mixed-gender ministry partnerships, and people have been equipped to form them, but there is little conviction behind the effort. Over time, this can be a recipe for disillusionment, and the project will wither.

Next, if the community culture domain is removed, people are both committed to forming flourishing mixed-gender partnerships and trained to make them happen, but the culture is not open to people expressing their convictions. It can be confusing and dissatisfying to repeatedly run into a wall, and that is what removing the community culture domain can feel like.

Lastly, removing the intentional practices domain would result in people who have a conviction about forming flourishing mixed-gender ministry

---

[7]One way that the interconnectedness of the model's attributes gets expressed in this book is through repeated cross-referencing. Often the reader will be directed to other chapters for related information.

partnerships situated in a culture that invites healthy activity, but no one knows how to capably form such partnerships. This lack of skills could end up resulting in a lot of talk with no accompanying action.

In the end, the Together in Ministry model looks like figure 1.5.

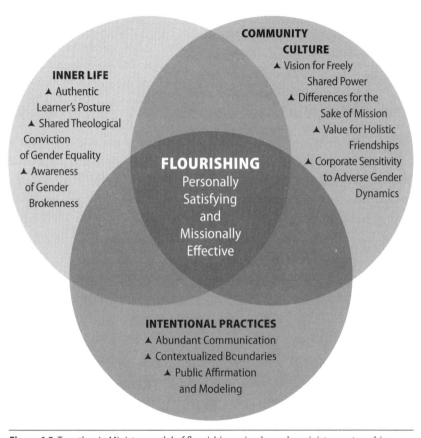

Figure 1.5. Together in Ministry model of flourishing mixed-gender ministry partnerships

FINAL THOUGHTS

Flourishing mixed-gender ministry partnerships will not happen by accident. On the contrary, they will take focused effort and courageous intentionality. Thankfully, the Together in Ministry model, with its ten attributes grouped into three domains, can help individuals and communities form flourishing mixed-gender ministry partnerships in greater measure.

PROCESSING QUESTIONS

1. Think of some of the mixed-gender ministry partnerships you have in your life. Which of the four quadrants would you put them in?

2. When have you experienced flourishing in the context of a mixed-gender ministry partnership? What specifically made it personally satisfying and missionally effective?

3. Go back through the brief introduction to the ten attributes. Give yourself a letter grade for each of the attributes. Which seem like strengths for you and the partnerships you are in? Which clearly need work?

4. As you sit with this overview of the Together in Ministry model, what questions do you have before you engage with each of the attributes in more detail?

PART 1

INNER LIFE

INNER LIFE
▲ Authentic Learner's Posture
▲ Shared Theological Conviction
of Gender Equality
▲ Awareness of Gender
Brokenness

THERE IS A WELL-WORN LITERARY PATHWAY connecting what is happening in a person's inner world with how they relate to the external world around them. For instance, Pete Scazzero notes that "if we do the hard work of integrating emotional health and spirituality, we can truly experience the wonderful promises God has given us—for our lives, churches, and communities."[1] Similarly, Ruth Haley Barton, writing from a leadership perspective, claims that "spiritual leadership emerges from our willingness to stay involved with our own soul."[2] Simply put, the state of a person's inner world will go a long way toward dictating how they engage with their environment.

Time and again, my research findings confirmed this truth in the area of mixed-gender ministry partnerships. If a person is developing in their inner life, there is a greater chance that they will be able to form a partnership that is personally satisfying and missionally effective. Who someone is, and is

---

[1]Pete Scazzero, *Emotionally Healthy Spirituality: It's Impossible to Be Spiritually Mature While Remaining Emotionally Immature* (Grand Rapids, MI: Zondervan, 2017), 19.
[2]Ruth Haley Barton, *Strengthening the Soul of Your Leadership: Seeking God in the Crucible of Ministry* (Downers Grove, IL: InterVarsity Press, 2018), 25.

becoming, matters a great deal when it comes to their capacity to contribute to a flourishing mixed-gender ministry partnership.

To be specific, three attributes fit into the domain of the inner life. First, when a person is able to cultivate an authentic learner's posture as they relate to others, they will be better equipped to develop a flourishing mixed-gender partnership. Next, a shared theological conviction of gender equality is a vital component to flourishing partnerships. Finally, the more self-aware a person is regarding their gender brokenness, the more they will be able to successfully navigate mixed-gender ministry partnerships. Part one will examine each of these three attributes in turn.

2

AUTHENTIC LEARNER'S POSTURE

LOOKING BACK ON MY RESEARCH PROCESS, I can recall a handful of times when an interview subject told me a story that really grabbed me. In those moments, my carefully constructed façade as a dispassionate observer fell away, and I could not hide my sense of wonder at what I was hearing.

In one such instance, a veteran minister recounted a story from earlier in his leadership experience. Single at the time, he found himself supervising several younger women who were newly pregnant. Upon hearing the news of their pregnancies, he visited his local bookstore and bought a number of books on pregnancy and motherhood, such as *What to Expect When You're Expecting*.

When I asked him about his motivation for doing this, he recalled his desire to more deeply understand what these women were about to experience, so that his supervision could be better informed and contextualized for these new mothers-to-be. Memorably, he told me that he read these books so that he could "have thoughtful conversations about childcare and breast-feeding needs at various team meetings."

There is something innately powerful about an authentic learner's posture. My research shows that when women and men cultivate and then exhibit such a posture in their relationships with one another, they are more likely to be able to form flourishing mixed-gender ministry partnerships.

LEARNER'S POSTURE IN THE RESEARCH

Many research participants testified to the importance of an authentic learner's posture in the mixed-gender partnerships they had experienced while in ministry. One person said, "You can't have good partnerships without both sides learning." To fill out this picture, respondents used phrases such as "walking in another person's shoes" and "getting into another person's world" to describe their experience.

Further, interviewees gave insight into four components that go into building and maintaining a learner's posture: humility, grace, a willingness to submit to one another, and curiosity. Humility is important in successfully stepping into another person's world. One participant modeled humility in the context of his interview when he shared examples of times that he had said unhelpful things that had prevented him from building healthy partnerships with women in his ministry context. Another interviewee remarked that "you have to know that you're going to have misses because you just didn't understand the other person."

As these two examples illustrate, consistently demonstrating a learner's posture can be difficult, and so several participants remarked about the need for grace. One said, "I think there also has to be an element of grace, because whenever you have crosscultural experiences, and I think gender can be a crosscultural experience, there are going to be mistakes, there are going to be things said or done that make the other person feel bad. To create the continued space for honesty and vulnerability to happen, you have to have grace and forgiveness as well."

Next, several participants said that a learner's posture includes a ready willingness to submit to their ministry partner's leadership or decision making. Reflecting on the importance of a learner's posture marked by this openness to submitting to others, one supervisor noted, "It is good to be in a position of deference." Another noted that "being in partnership means choosing to give up some of my power and prerogative."[1]

Finally, the theme of curiosity emerged again and again in the research. When invited to tell a story illustrating a flourishing mixed-gender ministry partnership in his life, one respondent lauded his ministry partner's curiosity: "The thing I have appreciated the most is how she is always ready with a question. That has helped me feel seen and known."

Each of these four elements—humility, grace, a willingness to submit to one another, and curiosity—require a high degree of personal maturity. Generally speaking, these things take effort to cultivate in our lives—they don't come automatically. The good news is that as we develop in these areas, we should find ourselves more able to adopt an authentic learner's

---

[1]In talking about a learner's posture, participants almost always referred to the interpersonal context. That is, they were talking specifically about walking in the shoes of a particular ministry partner. As this quote suggests, inhabiting a learner's posture could also extend beyond the boundaries of interpersonal relationships to seeking to understand systems, structures, and cultures (see chap. 8).

posture, and as a result, our mixed-gender ministry partnerships should be able to thrive.

JESUS AND A LEARNER'S POSTURE

To understand the value of an authentic learner's posture in the Scriptures, we need look no further than Jesus. In his ministry, Jesus placed a high value on seeking understanding by entering into another person's world and asking thoughtful questions, and he welcomed these same practices in others.

First, we see this general principle on display in Jesus' exhortation to his disciples to engage his parables with a learner's posture. In Mark 4:1-20, Jesus tells the parable of the sower to a "very large crowd." Later, when Jesus is alone, his disciples take the opportunity to ask him to explain the parable. Jesus judges their inquisitive response to be the appropriate one, as he exclaims, "To you has been given the secret of the kingdom of God, but for those outside, everything comes in parables" (Mark 4:11). While most of the people that day left their interaction with Jesus having heard a nice story about soils, those who employed a learner's posture were rewarded with an understanding of the parable's deeper meaning. For Jesus, an inner life marked by a robust learner's posture is a critical aspect of our discipleship.

In mixed-gender interactions, Jesus likewise affirmed the significance of an authentic learner's posture. For instance, Jesus affirmed Mary's choice to position herself at his feet in a learner's posture in Luke 10:38-42, a passage that will be examined in further depth in chapter six. Similarly, in his encounter with the woman at the well in John 4, Jesus confirmed the value of a learner's posture by dialoguing with this woman, answering three different questions she posed to him during their conversation by the well. In the end, the woman's learner's posture, coupled with Jesus' provocative answers to her questions, results in her learning Jesus' true identity. One commentator captures this woman's learner's posture and its implications this way: "thus the only pronouncement of Jesus' messiahship and an implicit identification of the Messiah with God is made to a woman, a non-Jew and a person of earthly disrepute, rather than to one of his own—because she is thirsty for that knowledge."[2]

---

[2]Kamila A. Blessing, "John," in *The IVP Women's Bible Commentary: An Indispensable Resource for All Who Want to View Scripture Through Different Eyes,* ed. Catherine Clark Kroeger and Mary J. Evans

In the Old Testament, the prophet Jeremiah speaks for the Lord, saying, "When you search for me, you will find me; if you seek me with all your heart" (Jeremiah 29:13). Even a cursory examination of Jesus' interaction with people in the Gospels demonstrates his agreement with this notion. Indeed, Jesus' repeated affirmation of an authentic learner's posture reminds us of its importance in every context, including that of mixed-gender ministry partnerships.

BENEFITS OF AN AUTHENTIC LEARNER'S POSTURE

Mixed-gender ministry partnerships marked by people who cultivate and exhibit an authentic learner's posture can experience the following four benefits. Each of these will make the experience of ministry partnership both personally satisfying and missionally effective.

To begin with, consistently walking in a ministry partner's shoes opens the door to greater relational trust. If you consider the people you trust the most in your life, it is likely also true that you know them the best (and vice versa) because you have made choices to walk in one another's shoes.

My friend Leslie and I worked together for years in ministry, and we spent plenty of time walking in each other's shoes, getting to know each other both in the ministry context and in our nonministry lives as well. Our experiences of getting to know one another resulted in a high degree of trust as well as a friendship, and so when it came time for my family to move to a different city, my wife, Amy, and I invited Leslie to come with us to help us during the moving process. Leslie jumped in, organizing our kitchen, watching our young son Josh, and providing the emotional support we needed as we made the move. Inviting Leslie into that transition moment was easy for us, largely because of the trust that had developed through an authentic learner's posture in both directions.

Next, knowing someone's story can inspire empathy. As we learn someone's story and experience, we often begin to care more deeply about them. Dr. Pascal Molenberghs, a professor of social neuroscience at the University of Melbourne, writes, "Empathy is important because it helps us understand how others are feeling so we can respond appropriately to the situation. It is typically associated with social behaviour and there is lots of research showing that

---

(Downers Grove, IL: InterVarsity Press, 2002), 598. As will be noted in chap. 10, there are reasons to believe that this woman was not, in fact, "a person of earthly disrepute."

greater empathy leads to more helping behaviour."[3] Empathy is a cornerstone of personally satisfying partnerships, and an authentic learner's posture is one way to develop empathy.

Third, when we walk in another person's shoes, we become able to more deeply understand our own experience. Both similarities and contrasts help bring clarity to our personal self-understanding. My ministry partner Layla and I have spent more than a decade working alongside one another, and we have been intentional about walking in one another's shoes. Looking at the world through Layla's eyes has helped me understand myself better. As just one example, I have often marveled at Layla's ability to surround herself with people. Relating to others is her power source. I tend to be the opposite, and so I have found greater clarity about my introverted temperament because I have spent time walking in Layla's extroverted shoes.

Fourth, the act of entering into another person's world can help them to feel seen and known. We live and minister in an era marked by what Pastor Sam Kim calls "an epidemic of loneliness." He writes, "At its deepest level, the human heart aches for relationship more than anything else. This is because God himself is a community within the fellowship of the Trinity. We desire to be in communion because before the advent of creation itself, God was part of an eternal fellowship. This ache in the human heart is clear residual evidence that we were created from community and for community."[4]

Cultivating and employing an authentic learner's posture allows us to meet this felt need in others, thus serving as an antidote to the problem of loneliness. When we ask questions and seek to understand another person's experience, we affirm their humanity. Each of these four benefits—increased relational trust, greater empathy, a clearer sense of our own experience, and the affirmation of another's humanity—are available to us as we embrace an authentic learner's posture in our mixed-gender ministry partnerships.

---

[3] Pascal Molenberghs, "Understanding Others' Feelings: What Is Empathy and Why Do We Need It?," *The Conversation*, January 8, 2017, https://theconversation.com/understanding-others -feelings-what-is-empathy-and-why-do-we-need-it-68494.

[4] Sam Kim, "Why the Current Loneliness Epidemic Is a Historical Gospel Opportunity," *The Exchange* (blog), February 20, 2020, www.christianitytoday.com/edstetzer/2020/february/why -current-loneliness-epidemic-is-historical-gospel-opport.html. In this quote, Kim uses masculine pronouns to refer to God, in contrast to the approach taken throughout this book.

BARRIERS TO AN AUTHENTIC LEARNER'S POSTURE

Unfortunately, consistently living out a learner's posture can be difficult. There are at least five barriers that can prevent people from developing an authentic learner's posture, specifically in the context of mixed-gender ministry partnerships.

First, our pride can prevent us from walking in another person's shoes. In *Mere Christianity*, C. S. Lewis vividly explains the danger of pride in the life of a Christian: "According to Christian teachers, the essential vice, the utmost evil, is Pride. Unchastity, anger, greed, drunkenness, and all that, are mere fleabites in comparison: it was through Pride that the devil became the devil: Pride leads to every other vice: it is the complete anti-God state of mind."[5] The problem with unchecked pride is that it can cause us to become overly focused on ourselves, and thus it can prevent us from even seeing the need to understand another person's experience.

Second, we can be too busy to really enter into another person's world. Cultivating a deeper understanding of another person's experience takes time, and too often we don't feel like we have it. Instead, we would rather offer a toss-away question along the lines of "How's it going?" anticipating the equally vacuous answer of "I'm fine."

But what if we chose to stop and really engage the people around us? What impact might we make on others, as well as ourselves, if we were to stop and ask a thoughtful question and followed that with an equally thoughtful reply? A "help me understand" type of question can make all the difference in communicating someone's value to us. Writing in *Psychology Today*, one therapist has noted, "Attention is the most basic form of love. Through it, we bless and are blessed."[6]

A third barrier to employing a learner's posture can be the fear of what we might learn if we do walk in our ministry partner's shoes. Taking on a learner's posture can expose us to our ministry partner's deep pain and sorrow. Indeed, walking in another person's shoes can mean that we are invited to understand both the good and the bad of their life experience. As Tish Harrison Warren notes, "My best friendships are with people who are willing to get in the muck with me, who see me as I am, and who speak to me of our hope in Christ in

---

[5]C. S. Lewis, *Mere Christianity* (New York: Harper One, 1980), 121-22.
[6]James V. Cordova, "Attention Is the Most Basic Form of Love," *Psychology Today* (blog), May 6, 2011, www.psychologytoday.com/us/blog/living-intimately/201105/attention-is-the-most-basic -form-love-2.

the midst of it."[7] This is a beautiful vision, but engaging someone's "muck" can be challenging.

Not long ago, I was invited to deliver a seminar about #MeToo and #ChurchToo at a Christian missions conference.[8] During my presentation, I discussed the importance of safe spaces, active listening, and thoughtful questions as we together deal with the scourge of gender-based violence in our communities of faith. When I finished my presentation, I was immediately given the opportunity to practice what I had just preached, as a long line of women (and some men) formed adjacent to the stage. For the next half hour, I listened and learned as person after person told me about how they had been abused by powerful men in their lives. After hearing each story, I would gently ask a question or two, and then some left with hugs, others with prayers.

While it was a privilege and an honor to be entrusted with the stories of these women and men, it was also emotionally taxing to be exposed to the raw pain that they were carrying. I had to both listen well and speak words that I hoped would bring healing and encouragement, but I left the stage that day emotionally exhausted. Taking on a learner's posture in the context of mixed-gender ministry partnerships can mean engaging with a person's deepest gender-related pain, and that is one reason why we may choose to not consistently inhabit such a posture.

Fourth, we can be reluctant to take on an authentic learner's posture because it often means we are invited to reciprocate. In other words, when you ask to walk in another person's shoes, you may well need to be prepared to allow them to walk in yours, and doing so can open us up to a level of vulnerability we are uncomfortable with.

Brené Brown describes vulnerability as "the birthplace of love, belonging, joy, courage, empathy, and creativity. It is the source of hope, empathy, accountability, and authenticity. If we want greater clarity in our purpose or deeper and more meaningful spiritual lives, vulnerability is the path."[9] To be sure, Brown's vision for vulnerability is compelling, but it can also be threatening, particularly for those who appreciate their privacy.

---

[7]Tish Harrison Warren, *Liturgy of the Ordinary: Sacred Practices in Everyday Life* (Downers Grove, IL: InterVarsity Press, 2019), 117.

[8]As I write, the #MeToo and #ChurchToo movements continue to actively call out sexual abuse and exploitation in a wide range of social contexts, including in the church. These movements will be referenced again in chaps. 4 and 9.

[9]Brené Brown, *Daring Greatly: How the Courage to Be Vulnerable Transforms the Way We Live, Love, Parent, and Lead* (New York: Avery, 2015), 34.

A fifth barrier to walking in another person's shoes can be the reality that certain topics tend to be considered off-limits in the context of mixed-gender ministry partnerships. For instance, in many pockets of Christian culture, talking about anything having to do with sex is judged to be taboo in mixed-gender settings. Adopting an authentic learner's posture will require a willingness to push through this culture of silence.

With that in mind, as we live out a learner's posture in our mixed-gender ministry partnerships, we will want to be thoughtful, particularly when talking about topics that have historically been off-limits. We should take it slow, seeking permission before asking questions that might make our ministry partners feel awkward, and we should employ all the hallmarks of good listening. For more on these tools, see chapter nine on communication.

Adopting an authentic learner's posture belongs in the inner life domain. It comes out of who we are. If we are not careful, these five barriers—personal pride, the time it can take to walk in our ministry partner's shoes, the fear of what we might learn, the concern about reciprocal vulnerability, and the reality that certain topics are considered off-limits—can thwart our development in this area.

CULTIVATING AN AUTHENTIC LEARNER'S POSTURE

The good news is that people involved in mixed-gender ministry partnerships can work to overcome these barriers and develop an authentic learner's posture in their inner lives. Four tactics for cultivating such a posture include asking for permission, asking thoughtful questions, choosing to listen, and reflecting on what you hear.

First, we should be diligent about asking for permission before walking in another person's shoes. Just because a learner's posture is a vital element of flourishing mixed-gender ministry partnerships doesn't mean we should bludgeon our way into another person's world. After all, they are still their shoes!

On more than one occasion, I have found myself sitting with one of the women who I have been blessed to partner with in ministry, and it has been clear that something in her life was amiss. And while everything in my pastoral heart wants to jump in and engage right away, I have learned (the hard way!) the value of asking for permission. A simple question such as "Would it be okay if I ask you a bit more about that?" can make all the difference in someone welcoming you into their experiences.

Second, we would be wise to ask thoughtful questions that lead to understanding. The woman at the well demonstrated her authentic learner's posture by asking Jesus her questions, and her engagement resulted in both greater understanding and a changed life. Placing ourselves in a learner's posture often involves deciding to engage with our ministry partners through well-thought-out questions.

When I was getting started in ministry, I was tasked with mentoring up-and-coming student leaders. As I started to lean into this assignment, it quickly dawned on me that I needed help knowing what to do in the actual meeting. Thankfully, I discovered the power of good questions. In her book *Disciplemaker's Handbook*, Alice Fryling writes, "The ability to ask good questions is a skill which is often untapped. In our society it is more common to hear people talking about themselves than asking questions of others. Self-absorbed people do not ask questions. If you are out of practice, if your capacity to ask loving questions has atrophied, here are some reminders: good questions are honest, appropriate, and open-ended."[10] Following this advice, I created a list of go-to questions that I would use every time I met with a student. All of a sudden, our conversations became lively and rich. As women and men partner together in the ministry context, they should likewise strive to become excellent question askers.[11]

Third, ministry partners should choose to listen. In her book *Life Together in Christ*, Ruth Haley Barton frames listening as an act of service, "the ability to simply listen and be with what is without having to fix, give advice or problem solve."[12] When we choose to listen to what our ministry partners are sharing with us, we serve them by giving them the gift of attention and presence.

With this in mind, perhaps the worst thing that ministry partners can do is to ask questions without really listening to the answers. If you have experienced this in your life, you know how off-putting it can be to be asked a question but not listened to as you reply. David Augsburger writes, "Being

---

[10]Alice Fryling, *Disciplemaker's Handbook: Helping People Grow in Christ* (Downers Grove, IL: Inter-Varsity Press, 1989), 76.

[11]For questions designed to help mixed-gender ministry partnerships flourish, see chaps. 9 and 10.

[12]Ruth Haley Barton, *Life Together in Christ: Experiencing Life Together in Community* (Downers Grove, IL: InterVarsity Press, 2014), 54.

heard is so close to being loved that for the average person they are almost indistinguishable. To say something you value deeply to another and to have him or her value it equally by listening to it carefully and appreciatively is the most universal way of exchanging social interest or demonstrating affection."[13] As we go about building flourishing mixed-gender ministry partnerships, we should strive to be fully present to our ministry partners in a posture of learning.

Fourth, after listening, a worthwhile practice is to make space to reflect on what we hear. Allowing ourselves to sit with a ministry partner's experience, through personal reflection, journaling, and intercession, has at least two benefits. First, it builds empathy in our hearts. When one of the women I work with shares her struggles with me and I make space to reflect and pray on what I hear, my heart bends toward her and her circumstances with empathy. Second, reflecting on what I hear affords me the opportunity to circle back around to my ministry partner, to check in with them about how they are doing, and this process can build relational trust.

Over the last year, I have been working with a woman named Destiny, and she has shared more than once about the challenges she has faced as a woman in ministry. I don't do this as often as I should in the mixed-gender ministry partnerships in my life, but recently I was praying for her in response to something I had heard in a prior conversation, and I sent her a quick text to check in. That text was hugely encouraging for her. When we take on a learner's posture and reflect on what we have heard, we can be a blessing to our ministry partners in this way.

FINAL THOUGHTS

During each research interview and focus group, I would prompt participants to list for me attributes of flourishing mixed-gender ministry partnerships. After taking a beat to reflect, one veteran leader answered, "I think it's the ability of both men and women to be able to describe the other person's reality."

What a beautiful picture that is—to know someone well enough to be able to fully articulate their reality. And one key to getting to that point is an authentic learner's posture that emerges from our inner world.

---

[13]David A. Augsburger, *Caring Enough to Hear and Be Heard* (Scottdale, PA: Regal, 1982), 12.

PROCESSING QUESTIONS

1. Can you think of a time someone from the opposite gender chose to walk in your shoes? What did they do? How did you feel?

2. What keeps you from exhibiting an authentic learner's posture in your mixed-gender ministry partnerships?

3. What are some go-to questions you could generate that would help you get to know your ministry partner's experience?

3

SHARED THEOLOGICAL CONVICTION
OF GENDER EQUALITY

NOT LONG INTO MY FIRST YEAR as an InterVarsity supervisor, I found myself in the midst of a fellowship-wide theological quagmire. At issue was the Bible's position on women in leadership; specifically, the question was whether the Bible dictated that leadership roles were reserved for men in the context of Christian ministry.

The students involved in our community were getting compelling teaching from two sides. On one hand, a lay pastor in a prominent local church was teaching a complementarian message in the church's college ministry.[1] According to this pastor, the Bible made it abundantly clear that men were called to lead and women were called to follow. On the other hand, our Inter-Varsity community read the Scriptures in a way that empowered women and men equally, with roles defined by gifting and calling instead of gender. In alignment with this egalitarian theological understanding, our practice included women regularly speaking at fellowship meetings and women and men sharing leadership in a variety of settings.

For me and my leadership, the clash of these two theological positions resulted in a long string of meetings with students who were concurrently involved in both ministries. Understandably, they were confused! As a leader, my job was to pastor them into and through the Scriptures.

On one occasion, I was sitting with a student leader in the campus library. This student was one of my favorites, primarily because he had been one of several mentored by my wife, Amy, during the prior academic year. In fact, at

---

[1]Complementarian theology places men in positions of leadership and authority, both in the church and in the home. Its theological foil, egalitarianism, affirms the full and equal partnership of women and men in the church and in the home. Our InterVarsity community operated with an egalitarian reading of the Scriptures.

the end of the previous year, this student had given Amy the gift that all leaders long to hear when he told her that he had grown more under her leadership than any prior year in his life with God.

Now, six months on from that statement, this student was describing his process of coming to embrace the complementarian theology of this church's college group. As we talked, he went on for a while, describing his newfound theological understanding that God's design was that men were to be leaders and women were to be followers.

When he finished his story, I asked him the question that I'd been eager to ask him since we first sat down. I said, "I know what you told Amy last year—that you had grown more under her leadership than any prior year in your life with God. In light of your newfound theological understanding, how are you interpreting your experience from last year?" He sat back and considered his answer, then looked at me and said, "That was God using Amy in spite of her disobedience."

Our theology matters, primarily because it so often serves as the lens through which we interpret our world. Time and again in the research process, a person's theology about women and men in ministry partnership was referenced as a critical factor in flourishing mixed-gender ministry partnerships. To be specific, when there is a shared conviction that the Bible affirms the Genesis vision for the full and equal partnership of women and men in ministry, flourishing mixed-gender ministry partnerships are more likely to become a reality.

A SHARED CONVICTION OF GENDER EQUALITY IN THE RESEARCH

This attribute, among the most cited in the research, was manifest in three ways. First, interviewees affirmed the importance of both ministry partners being on the same page theologically. Second, the consensus was that that page needs to articulate a theology that affirms the full and equal partnership of women and men in the context of ministry. Finally, respondents described this attribute using the language of "conviction."

To begin with, my research suggests that both members in the partnership should have a shared interpretation of the Scriptures in this area. This makes sense intuitively; after all, it would be difficult to partner with someone of the opposite gender if that person held a contrasting or competing theology about the roles of women and men in ministry. In one interview, a leader explained that "for partnership to be successful . . . there has to be theological agreement on men and women doing ministry [and] working together." In a separate interview, a female respondent put it more bluntly, noting that "it is impossible for me to partner with someone that has a restrictive theological position."[2]

Next, participants repeatedly stressed the importance of partners sharing an understanding that the Bible advocates for the full and equal partnership of women and men in the context of ministry. Reflecting on what this shared theology should entail, one veteran leader labeled it as a "conviction that God and Scripture honor these kinds of relationships, that this is pretty much a part of what God calls us to be, [and that this is a] biblical calling, not just a politically correct thing." This shared theological understanding harmonizes with Carol Becker's assertion in *Becoming Colleagues*, where a shared belief in the viability of mixed-gender partnerships is considered essential for partnership: "Mixed-gender teams will not work unless we believe in them. This requires believing that women as well as men should be leaders. It also requires believing that women can be equal partners with men in leadership."[3]

Finally, when respondents talked about this attribute, they used the language of conviction. In one case, an interviewee insisted that it wasn't enough for ministry partners to share a "working or pragmatic value"; instead, conviction is required. The notion of conviction couples belief with a commitment to action, and for the participants surveyed the sentiment seemed to be that if partnerships are going to persevere in the midst of difficulty, people must not only have done the theological work in this area but they must have backed up that conceptual work with concrete deeds done from a place of conviction. Memorably, one woman concluded that she would only partner with a man if she could see from his actions that he was "down with the cause."

These three components, then, undergird this critical attribute. When partners share a theological conviction that God's design is for the full and equal partnership of women and men in the ministry context, their ministry partnerships are more likely to become places of flourishing.

---

[2]I choose to use the word *female* as an adjective at points in this book, but there is a bit of a debate whether to use *female* or *woman* in these cases. For more on this topic, see Mary Norris, "Female Trouble: The Debate over 'Woman' as an Adjective," *The New Yorker*, May 30, 2019, www.newyorker.com/culture/comma-queen/female-trouble-the-debate-over-woman-as-an-adjective.

[3]Carol Becker, *Becoming Colleagues: Women and Men Serving Together in Faith* (San Francisco: Jossey-Bass, 2000), 84. Becker's rubric details nine criteria of flourishing mixed-gender partnerships: reflecting, learning, believing, naming, including, communicating, working, influencing, and modeling.

A DEVELOPING CONVICTION IN THE APOSTLE PAUL

How might a person develop a conviction that the Bible affirms the full and equal partnership of women and men in ministry? Perhaps the apostle Paul can provide an example for us, as his theological journey to a place of conviction about gender equality was anything but a given, particularly in light of where he started.[4]

The Scriptures tell us that Paul started out his public life as Saul, a Pharisee who was committed to snuffing out the nascent movement of Christianity. In fact, we first meet Saul in Acts 8:1, when he is introduced as one who endorsed the stoning of Stephen, one of the early leaders in the church. Luke tells us that "Saul was ravaging the church by entering house after house; dragging off both men and women, he committed them to prison" (Acts 8:3).

Given that Saul is identified as a particularly militant Pharisee, it is reasonable to assume that he would have habitually prayed one of the liturgical prayers of this day: "Blessed are you Lord our God, King of the Universe, who has not made me a gentile. Blessed are you Lord our God, King of the Universe, who has not made me a slave. Blessed are you Lord our God, King of the Universe, who has not made me a woman."[5] Imagine regularly reciting that prayer! With the misogyny embedded in that prayer, how could Saul *not* develop the conviction that men were more important than women?

Of course, everything in Saul's life gets completely upended on the road to Damascus (Acts 9:1-19). In a miraculous encounter with Jesus, Saul is confronted about his persecution of Jesus' followers and sent to be mentored by Ananias and later by Barnabas. In fact, Acts 11:26 tells us that Saul spent a year learning from Barnabas and the first Christians in Antioch. And while we don't know much about the specifics of what that season of study and discipleship entailed, we do get a glimpse of its fruit.

---

[4]Credit to April Fiet, copastor of First Presbyterian Church in Scotts Bluff, Nebraska, for this insight, from a message she delivered at a Building God's Church Together event for the Reformed Church in America in Ames, Iowa in February 2019. For more on April's ministry, see www.aprilfiet.com.

[5]David Instone-Brewer cites the traditional Jewish prayer book for this particular prayer, and he notes that Jewish men would pray this just before the morning Shema. Interestingly, Instone-Brewer also points out that the Greeks had a similar blessing: "[Socrates] used to say there are three blessings for which he was grateful to Fortune: first that I was born a human being and not one of the brutes; next that I was born a man and not a woman; thirdly a Greek and not a barbarian." Tragically, misogyny has deep roots in our philosophy as well as in our theology and ecclesiology. *Traditions of the Rabbis from the Era of the New Testament: Prayer and Agriculture*, vol. 1 (Grand Rapids, MI: Eerdmans, 2004), 79.

In particular, we know that Paul experienced some sort of transformation regarding his theological understanding of women and men in ministry. As noted in the introduction to this book, Paul is the one who wrote that "there is no longer Jew or Greek, there is no longer slave or free, there is no longer male and female; for all of you are one in Christ Jesus" (Galatians 3:28). Embedded in this egalitarian statement is an intriguing bit of symmetry, as it directly overturns the three social divisions expressed in the liturgical prayer referenced earlier. Reflecting on the link between that prayer and Galatians 3:28, Marg Mowczko writes, "Paul . . . chose to use the same three categories of humanity, in the same order, to highlight that these social distinctions are irrelevant if we are in Christ. Whatever our gender and whatever our race, we are all [children] of God and we are all Abraham's offspring and heirs. This is our true identity, and this truth should inform our worldview."[6] Paul's transformed worldview certainly included the theological truth that women were equal to men.

To go one step further, we can see that Paul's theological conviction, so vividly expressed in Galatians 3:28, found tangible expression in his daily ministry work. As many of the chapters in this book will attest, mixed-gender ministry partnerships were normative and vital for Paul. Ministry partnerships with women such as Phoebe, Lydia, Junia, and Priscilla illustrate Paul's consistent and faithful practice. Truly, Paul's belief in the full and equal partnership between women and men in the context of ministry was matched by his actions, and that, again, is the stuff of conviction.

All in all, Paul's theological journey in this area should give us hope. While some will experience a theological journey that takes them to where the student mentioned in the beginning of this chapter ended up, others can and will travel the same path as Paul. As they develop a theology that supports the full and equal partnership of women and men in ministry, and as they share that with others in partnership, they can find themselves experiencing the joy of flourishing mixed-gender ministry partnerships.

BENEFITS OF A SHARED CONVICTION OF GENDER EQUALITY

As people do the work to develop a theological conviction such as the one articulated in the research, they can expect to experience several benefits. First, while each attribute in this model is important, this one in many ways serves

---

[6]Marg Mowczko, "Galatians 3:28: Our Identity in Christ & in the Church," *Marg Mowczko* (blog), December 12, 2013, https://margmowczko.com/galatians-3_28-identity/.

as a foundation for the rest. For example, it would be impossible to embrace and successfully live out a vision for freely shared power (see chap. 5) if one's theological understanding grants more power to men than women. Or modeling and publicly affirming the full partnership of women and men in ministry (see chap. 11) doesn't make sense apart from a theology that supports such a thing. Sometimes when I present on this model, people will ask me if any of the attributes are dealbreakers. In my view, this one comes the closest.

Second, there is inherent value in being on the same theological page with a ministry partner. Church history is replete with communities bound together by various creeds and theological statements. To be theologically aligned permits mixed-gender ministry partners to experience the unity evocatively described in Psalm 133,

> How very good and pleasant it is
> when kindred live together in unity!
> It is like the precious oil on the head,
> running down upon the beard,
> on the beard of Aaron,
> running down over the collar of his robes.
> It is like the dew of Hermon,
> which falls on the mountains of Zion.
> For there the LORD ordained his blessing,
> life forevermore.

This beautiful and compelling picture of unity is available to women and men in the context of their ministry partnerships, provided they are on the same page theologically.[7]

Third, sharing a conviction in the full and equal partnership of women and men in ministry grants mixed-gender ministry partners permission to actually live out the partnership envisioned in Genesis. Leadership coach Sue Wigston writes,

> Conviction allows individuals and teams to overcome obstacles when they arise because they have a strong belief in what they're doing, regardless of the struggles and challenges faced along the way. Without this conviction,

---

[7]The imagery in Psalm 133 paints a picture of abundance, of anointing oil drenching the priest and of dew covering the holy mountains of Israel. "The psalm's similes suggest that brotherly unity is an epiphanic experience, combining calling, holiness, life and power." Leland Ryken, James C. Wilhoit, and Tremper Longman III, eds., *Dictionary of Biblical Imagery* (Downers Grove, IL: InterVarsity Press, 1998), 126.

obstacles can quickly become permanent barriers to success. Conviction also sparks passion, which is a great energizer because passion and energy are infectious to those around you. Conviction helps overcome resistance, both external and internal. Resistance comes in many forms, but having a foundation of conviction allows you to persevere in the face of it.[8]

Conviction is a powerful tool. Shared conviction can provide the impetus to try out mixed-gender ministry partnerships, particularly in a context where they are countercultural. In the partnerships that I have experienced, there has almost always been this shared theological conviction, and we have therefore felt the freedom to boldly live it out.

BARRIERS TO A SHARED CONVICTION OF GENDER EQUALITY

Before discussing how to develop the kind of theological conviction that marked the finish line of Paul's journey, we must examine the barriers to developing such an understanding. First, it must be noted that the default theological position in most churches runs contrary to the Genesis understanding of gender equality that was repeatedly affirmed in the research. Too many of our churches and communities continue to embody a theology that restricts the full participation of women in leadership. And while we can hope that no pastors are waking each morning with that first-century misogynistic prayer on their lips, it remains true that a restrictive theological bias perpetuates a system that relegates women to the margins of church life.

In his 2012 book *The Resignation of Eve,* Jim Henderson cites a Barna study that noted a 20 percent drop in church participation by women over the prior twenty years. In reflecting on potential explanations for this, Henderson concludes that a lack of authoritative leadership opportunities has essentially made the church an increasingly hostile environment for women, causing them to resign from the local church in these historic numbers. "A significant number [of women] are frustrated because they can't lead at all [in the church] or are not allowed to lead within their areas of giftedness."[9]

[8]Sue Wigston, "Why Great Leadership Requires Conviction," *Eagle's Flight* (blog), January 17, 2019, www.eaglesflight.com/blog/why-great-leadership-requires-conviction.
[9]Jim Henderson, *The Resignation of Eve: What If Adam's Rib Is No Longer Willing to Be the Church's Backbone?* (Ventura, CA: Barna, 2012), 9. Henderson talks about "resignation" in three ways. First, women have resigned themselves to subordinate positions in the local church and basically acquiesced to the status quo. Next, women have resigned from the church entirely or found a different church that allows them to use their gifts. Finally, women have resigned in the sense that they have decided to stay within the church and advocate for a greater openness for themselves and other women.

Because the default theological position continues to place limitations on the roles available to women in leadership, embracing a theological conviction of gender equality means swimming against the theological current. This is always a difficult process.[10]

A second barrier is that deeply held beliefs can be difficult to change. With the church's default setting being what it is, significant effort will be required to shift people's theological perspectives. In an attempt to understand how to help someone change such beliefs, sociologist Jack Mezirow articulated what he labeled Transformative Learning Theory: "Transformative learning may be defined as learning that transforms problematic frames of reference to make them more inclusive, discriminating, reflective, open, and emotionally able to change."[11] According to Mezirow, this transformational learning journey is a tenfold process:

- A disorienting dilemma

- Self-examination with feelings of guilt or shame

- A critical assessment of assumptions

- Recognition that one's discontent and process of transformation are shared and that others have negotiated a similar change

- Exploration of options for new roles, relationships, and actions

- Planning of a course of action

- Acquisition of knowledge and skills for implementing one's plans

- Provisionally trying out new roles

- Building of competence and self-confidence in new roles and relationships

- A reintegration into one's life on the basis of conditions dictated by one's new perspective.[12]

My friend Kevin's theological journey fits Mezirow's model well. At one point in his life, Kevin held a complementarian theological position. When

---

[10]To be sure, "swimming against the theological current" will look different for women and men. For many women, this is a theological quest for full dignity and access. Men, who have historically benefited from a theology that automatically grants both dignity and access, will need to engage a theology that includes women as equals. To use a metaphor, as the church builds a bigger table, women will need to discern what it means to sit there, and men will need to discern how to share the space.

[11]Jack Mezirow and Edward W. Taylor, *Transformative Learning Theory in Practice: Insights from Community, Workplace, and Higher Education* (San Francisco, CA: Jossey-Bass, 2009), 22. Credit to Leanne Dzubinski for introducing me to Transformative Learning Theory. For an overview of her work on unconscious gender bias, see chap. 8.

[12]Mezirow and Taylor, *Transformative Learning Theory*, 19.

he got involved in an InterVarsity community that modeled egalitarian theology, he met his disorienting dilemma. After a robust inner journey, he found himself investigating new ways of thinking and functioning through both mentoring and intensive Bible study in community. Ultimately, Kevin tried on a new theological position and it fit him. Today, he is a committed egalitarian who believes that "God's intent is for women and men to live in harmony, to be equal partners and costewards of world that God created."[13] As Kevin's story illustrates, deeply held beliefs can change, but that change takes effort.

Third, proper theological exploration takes time, which can be in short supply in our churches. This is particularly true when a theology is disputed, as it often is with topics at the intersection of gender and faith. In Kevin's case, this was a four-year journey. So many topics vie for attention in our church agendas, it can be difficult to make and protect space for this kind of theological exploration.[14]

Not long ago, a pastor friend asked me to consult with his leadership team as they considered a theological switch from complementarianism to egalitarianism. At our first meeting together, I painted a picture of what I thought such a process should entail, including individual and communal study, working together on a theological statement, meetings with various constituencies, and a thorough reexamination of the culture and structures of the church. In the end, they decided that the process that I laid out was more than they could take on at the moment, and this seems to be fairly typical. Available bandwidth is an issue in most communities of faith.

A fourth barrier to embracing a theology of women and men in full and equal partnership is the pushback that can come with a shift in theology.

---

[13]In response to his conviction, Kevin has become a good example of someone who is a male ally to women. I have articulated a developmental pathway for raising up male allies; see Rob Dixon, "Raising Up Allies: A Standardized Pathway for Developing Men into Allies to Women," *Priscilla Papers*, July 31, 2020, www.cbeinternational.org/resource/article/priscilla-papers-academic-journal/raising-allies-standardized-pathway-developing. For more on the notion of male allyship, see David G. Smith and W. Brad Johnson, *Good Guys: How Men Can Be Better Allies for Women in the Workplace* (Boston: Harvard Business Review Press, 2020).
[14]Barna's 2019 *State of the Bible* report noted two discouraging shifts regarding overall biblical literacy. First, the percentage of "Bible Centered adults" has declined from 9 percent to 5 percent. Second, 35 percent of adults reported never using the Bible in 2019, a 10 percent increase over eight years. If these trends continue, they will further complicate this particular barrier, as biblical literacy will continue to be supplanted by culturally prescribed understandings of the Bible's message regarding gender equality. Barna Group, *State of the Bible 2019: Trends in Engagement*, April 18, 2019, www.barna.com/research/state-of-the-bible-2019.

Indeed, theological opposition can keep people from entering into a process that results in a changed position.

In the same season that I engaged with that student in the library, I also encountered the most intense theological pushback I have ever received. One day, I arrived at the student union for a similar meeting with a student only to quickly realize that he wasn't alone. Sitting next to my student was the very lay pastor that was promoting the complementarian message in that local church. Upon noticing him, my heart sank, as I knew the next hour would be difficult.

And indeed it was. Though I had done a decent amount of theological reflection and exploration, it wasn't nearly enough. That pastor spent the hour eviscerating each of my arguments, repeatedly labeling me a "false teacher." I left the meeting incredibly discouraged, and it took a crew of friends to put me back together again. The reality of pushback can be a real roadblock to theological change in this area.

Each of these four barriers—an oppositional theological current, the complexity of changing our entrenched perspectives, insufficient time or capacity to engage in a process of theological reflection, and the possibility of pushback—can keep individuals as well as communities from developing a conviction that God's design is for the full and equal partnership of women and men in the ministry context.

HOW TO DEVELOP A SHARED CONVICTION OF GENDER EQUALITY

In this chapter, I have already alluded to how we can develop a theological conviction marked by the full and equal partnership of women and men in ministry. First and foremost, communities must create safe spaces for people to explore their theology in the context of community.

In the wake of my encounter with that student in the library, I realized that we had a problem in our InterVarsity community. While we were providing our people with a robust experience of mixed-gender ministry partnership, our theological equipping wasn't keeping pace.[15] This resulted in students

---

[15]This is not just my observation. More than once in an interview, a participant would describe the low level of theological acuity around them. For instance, one respondent said, "The weird thing is that I don't think [women and men in ministry partnership] is something we've taught; I think it has just been organically modeled." No matter your theological background or position, there will be room for more study and reflection. That is true for egalitarians and complementarians as well as those in the middle.

graduating from our InterVarsity communities with nothing but anecdotal or experiential evidence to support their beliefs that women and men were designed to partner. Inevitably, they would encounter pushback after they had graduated, and when that happened, they would find themselves underequipped theologically.

As a way to address this deficit, and in a spirit of repentance, my colleague Tina and I created a week-long theological training course called "Women in the Bible." In the seminar, we spend each morning and afternoon studying the entire Bible, starting in Genesis and ending in the Epistles. In the evenings, we turn our hearts and minds toward application, engaging our own worldviews, life in our communities, and the plight of women in the world.

Each time we have hosted the seminar, it has been a powerful experience, but it has also been costly. Doing this seminar has meant that people could not take other relevant seminars. Also, challenging deeply held perspectives takes a lot of work, and at points people have left the seminar with more questions than answers. Still, the experience of exploring both theology and practice in a safe context has been invaluable for our community. In part due to this seminar, increasingly we are now sending graduates who have done their theological homework into new faith communities.

Communities must discern ways to create and then protect space for people to wrestle with their theology of women and men in ministry partnerships. These venues should be well led, resource rich, and, above all else, open and curious spaces. One practical way to do this is to host a book group, using one of the books referenced at the end of this chapter.

FINAL THOUGHTS

In the aftermath of both the disorienting experiences referenced in this chapter, I launched into a season of focused theological reflection. I read everything I could get my hands on, talked with anyone who would listen, and carefully and methodically worked out my theological position. In the process, my level of conviction increased significantly, to the point where I began to go on the offensive; if a person didn't agree with my egalitarian theological conviction, we were going to have problems.

One day, I was driving with a mentor, expressing how important this topic had become in my life and leadership. When I was done, he looked at me and said, "Rob, you're becoming like that pastor. It's important that you learn how to hold your convictions with humility." That word pierced my heart. Having a conviction is important, but how we hold our convictions is just as, if not more, important.

Like myself, like the apostle Paul, like Kevin, and like my organization, we all have room to grow in our theology of women and men in ministry partnerships. There will always be more to learn. The importance of a shared theological conviction in the full and equal partnership of women and men in the ministry context is clear. The only question is, Will we make space to engage with the Scriptures and with one another in this area?

PROCESSING QUESTIONS

1. What is your theology of women and men in ministry partnership?

2. Who or what have been your biggest theological influences?

3. What outstanding theological questions do you have?

4. What would a faithful next step look like for you to develop your theological fluency on this subject?

There are plenty of useful resources on the theology of gender equality. For a comparative examination of complementarianism and egalitarianism, consider

Gundry, Stanley, and James R. Beck, eds. *Two Views on Women in Ministry*. rev. ed. Grand Rapids, MI: Zondervan, 2005.

For a comprehensive overview of the egalitarian theological position, consider

Mathews, Alice. *Gender Roles and the People of God: Rethinking What We Were Taught About Men and Women in the Church*. Grand Rapids, MI: Zondervan, 2016.

Peppiatt, Lucy. *Rediscovering Scripture's Vision for Women: Fresh Perspectives on Disputed Texts*. Downers Grove, IL: InterVarsity Press, 2019.

Pierce, Ronald W., and Rebecca Merrill Groothuis, eds. *Discovering Biblical Equality: Complementarity Without Hierarchy*. Downers Grove, IL: InterVarsity Press, 2004.

Several online resources offer shorter treatments of the theological issues about women and men in leadership. See, for instance, thejuniaproject.com, cbeinternational.org, and margmowczko.com.

4

AWARENESS OF GENDER BROKENNESS

The notion of self-awareness has been in vogue for at least twenty-four hundred years. In fact, the ancient Greeks developed the maxim "know thyself" to capture the importance of this idea of self-knowledge. Historians are not certain of the phrase's precise origin, but Greek writer Pausanias notes that the phrase was one of two "celebrated maxims" that graced the forecourt of the Temple of Apollo at Delphi, dating to the fourth century BCE.[1]

Over time, this ancient call to self-awareness made its way into Greek literature. For instance, the playwright Aeschylus used the phrase in his play *Prometheus Bound*, when Oceanus exhorts a shackled Prometheus using the words.[2] Later, Plato explored the virtue of self-knowledge in several of his writings. In one case, Plato imagines his mentor Socrates saying, "But I have no leisure for them at all; and the reason, my friend, is this: I am not yet able, as the Delphic inscription has it, to know myself; so it seems to me ridiculous, when I do not yet know that, to investigate irrelevant things."[3]

Through the centuries, other writers and thinkers have taken their cue from the Greeks and explored this theme of self-awareness. Thomas Hobbes referenced a version of the phrase in his 1651 work *The Leviathan;*[4] Ralph Waldo Emerson wrote a poem titled "Know Thyself";[5] and Flannery O'Connor wrote, "To know oneself is, above all, to know what one lacks. It is to measure

---

[1]Pausanias, *Description of Greece* 10.24. The other inscription read "nothing in excess."
[2]Aeschylus, *Prometheus Bound* 309.
[3]Plato, *Phaedrus* 229e, in *Plato in Twelve Volumes*, translated by Harold N. Fowler, vol. 9 (Cambridge, MA: Harvard University Press, 1925).
[4]Thomas Hobbes, *Leviathan*, ed. Richard Tuck, rev. student ed. (New York: Cambridge University Press, 1996), 10. Hobbes actually uses the phrase "*Nosce teipsum*," which he translates, "Read thyself."
[5]Emerson's poem is actually titled "Gnothi Seauton," which is a transliteration of the Greek words for "know thyself."

oneself against Truth, and not the other way around. The first product of self-knowledge is humility."[6]

More recently, Christian thought leaders have applied the notion of self-awareness to the discipleship process. For instance, in *The Gift of Being Yourself*, David Benner writes, "The goal of the spiritual journey is the transformation of self. . . . This requires knowing both our self and God. Both are necessary if we are to discover our true identity as those who are 'in Christ,' because the self is where we meet God. Both are also necessary if we are to live out the uniqueness of our vocation."[7]

The individuals interviewed for this project affirm this historic emphasis on self-awareness. When a person's inner world includes a healthy and growing sense of self-awareness, particularly in the area of gender brokenness, they are more likely to be able to contribute to flourishing mixed-gender ministry partnerships.

SELF-AWARENESS IN THE RESEARCH

In the research, a significant cross section of participants acknowledged the importance of pursuing self-awareness, specifically in the area of gender brokenness. Capturing the spirit of the larger pool of input, one person said, "I definitely think that the way we feel and think about and deal with sexuality is really important when it comes to relationships with men and women, because I think some people are wanting to be so careful to be far back from the line of anything that would be below reproach, or maybe they're afraid of themselves and their own stumbles . . . that I think if people aren't dealing with that in their lives it's going to impact our relationships as men and women."

Next, though the notion of self-awareness is fairly straightforward, it raises the question of what exactly people need to become aware of. By way of definition, "gender brokenness" refers to areas of struggle in our lives that stem from our experience as women or men. In their interviews, respondents detailed a number of examples of brokenness around gender.

---

[6]Flannery O'Connor, *Mystery and Manners: Occasional Prose* (New York: Farrar, Straus and Giroux, 1969), 35.
[7]David G. Benner, *The Gift of Being Yourself: The Sacred Call to Self-Discovery* (Downers Grove, IL: Inter-Varsity Press, 2004), 14. Other notable thinkers that have encouraged self-awareness in the context of a person's spiritual journey include Dallas Willard, Ruth Haley Barton, Pete Scazzero, Janet Hagberg, and Robert Guelich.

For instance, men interviewed for this project mentioned issues such as lust, the consumption of pornography, and the objectification of women as examples of gender brokenness. When these things are unaddressed, they can cause havoc, both internally and in relationships with female ministry partners. In addition, one supervisor mentioned the impediment of unaware men "not knowing how much space they are taking up in a given situation." In this way, gender brokenness is more than just sexual brokenness; it also includes how we manage ourselves as gendered beings in communal settings.[8]

Many female participants talked about the painful effects of being chronically undervalued and objectified. Some talked about struggling with self-image and of being hesitant or fearful around men. In her interview, one female leader expressed her wish that "women [would] understand how gender has affected them, and how that affects their ability to value themselves and bring their full self in given situations."

Bias against the other gender is another way that gender brokenness can manifest, and both women and men shared examples of growing in awareness of their gender biases. For example, several interviewees related stories about people assuming that the male partners were leaders and the female partners were executive assistants, even when the opposite was actually true. Reflecting on where he began in his journey of awareness about his biases, one male leader said, "Unawareness is a block, particularly when men are oblivious. Though they mean well, they just don't get it." Similarly, a female interviewee reported that "not realizing you have a bias or a prejudice can be detrimental."[9]

Overall, the consensus from the research is that gender brokenness is a reality that everyone experiences. Though it can play out differently for women and men, the critical question is whether or not a person is aware of their brokenness. An ever-developing self-awareness is vital if someone is going to move toward wholeness and then be able to engage in a flourishing mixed-gender ministry partnership.

SELF-AWARENESS IN THE SCRIPTURES

The virtue of self-awareness is likewise highlighted in the Scriptures. The cautionary tale of King David offers perhaps the most vivid depiction of the

---

[8]For more on the concept of taking up space, see chap. 5.
[9]A litany of examples of unconscious gender bias can be found in chap. 8.

importance of self-awareness, specifically in the area of gender brokenness. David was Israel's paradigmatic king, a "man after God's own heart."[10] But, tragically, at the beginning of his reign David lacked self-awareness regarding his gender brokenness. The text in 2 Samuel 11–12 recounts the story of his most heinous moral lapse.

The passage begins with David lounging on the palace rooftop, the wrong place for him to be when his army was at war.[11] Gazing toward the roof of a nearby house, David notices Bathsheba taking a bath. Overcome with lust, David summons and then sexually exploits Bathsheba.[12] After Bathsheba gets pregnant, David seeks to cover up the episode, first by trying to have her husband Uriah sleep with her, and then by conspiring to have Uriah killed in battle. In the end, David is confronted with his sins by the prophet Nathan, who lays out the consequences, which include the loss of David and Bathsheba's baby. Ultimately, David's actions decimate not only his own life but those of Uriah, Bathsheba, and the young child. Appropriately, this scandal wrecked David. His immediate response is to lament, and in 2 Samuel 12:13 he declares, "I have sinned against the LORD."

David's exploitation of Bathsheba and his subsequent attempt to cover it up are ultimately what bring God's punishment, but David's lack of self-awareness is what starts him down the path to ruin. From the moment he scanned the rooftops from atop his palace, David was clearly disconnected from his inner world. As a result, his brokenness, manifest both in his lust and in the toxic leveraging of his royal power, guides his actions. Commentator Joyce Baldwin writes, "From all that the reader has seen of David thus far, he was not a callous man; but he was capable of falling to unsuspected depths of evil at a whim, so within one and the same person two people were

---

[10]In Samuel's rebuke to then King Saul, the prophet refers to the next king as "a man after [God's] own heart" (1 Samuel 13:14).

[11]"Kings, because of the duties of state or physical reasons, could not always accompany the army in every campaign," but, in this case, the text makes it clear that David made a poor choice. John H. Walton, Victor H. Matthews, and Mark W. Chavalas, *The IVP Bible Background Commentary: Old Testament* (Downers Grove, IL: InterVarsity Press, 2000), 337.

[12]There can be some dispute about how to label what happens between David and Bathsheba. Some might consider the encounter an "affair," while others would label it as "rape." There is ample evidence to suggest the latter is the more appropriate reading of the text, primarily because of the social power disparity that existed between David and Bathsheba. "For [Bathsheba] it would have been impossible to resist the advances of a man in such a powerful position, a man who was capable of taking whatever and whomever he wanted." Joy Osgood, *1 & 2 Samuel*, in *The IVP Women's Bible Commentary*, ed. Catherine Clark Kroeger and Mary J. Evans (Downers Grove, IL: InterVarsity Press, 2002), 175.

struggling for supremacy."[13] Tragically, unaware of what was happening in his inner world, the wrong version of David won out that evening on the palace roof.

In the end, faced with the consequences of both his lack of self-awareness and his gender brokenness, David turns to the Lord. In his confessional words recorded in Psalm 51, we observe the beginning of David's journey toward authentic self-knowledge. Among the words of confession and repentance is this plea: "You desire truth in the inward being; / therefore teach me wisdom in my secret heart" (Psalm 51:6). At the core of David's confession is a plea for greater self-awareness. In his commentary, James H. Waltner notes that Psalm 51:6 "expresses the painful realization of the gap between God's demands and the sinner's state, inviting introspection to ponder one's self before God."[14]

The unaware and broken David loitering on the palace rooftop when he should have been leading the nation into battle would have been a poor candidate for a flourishing mixed-gender ministry partnership. But perhaps the chastened David, who in his despair penned Psalm 51:6, would be a different story.[15] Indeed, having a deeper level of self-awareness might well have helped him avoid the sin with Bathsheba altogether.

BENEFITS OF INCREASING SELF-AWARENESS

There are at least three benefits that come with developing self-awareness in the context of flourishing mixed-gender ministry partnerships. First, a healthy sense of self-awareness around gender brokenness sets up several of the other attributes in this model. For instance, when mixed-gender ministry partners sit down to have a conversation about contextualized boundaries (see chap. 10), an awareness of their personal journeys in the area of gender brokenness will come in handy.

One pastor I know has a history that includes a moral lapse. Like David, inattention to his internal world resulted in a series of bad decisions that ended up disqualifying him from ministry for a season. Thankfully, he responded by

[13]Joyce G. Baldwin, *1 & 2 Samuel: An Introduction & Commentary*, Tyndale Old Testament Commentaries (Downers Grove, IL: InterVarsity Press, 1988), 242.

[14]James H. Waltner, *Psalms*, Believers Church Bible Commentary (Scottdale, PA: Herald, 2006), 258.

[15]The "perhaps" here is crucial. Repentance is a key part of a healing journey, but it is not the only part. Just because a leader has expressed repentance does not mean they should automatically be restored to leadership. Instead, careful discernment is required to determine if or when a person is ready to resume ministry leadership, particularly in mixed-gender contexts.

giving serious attention to pursuing self-discovery and wholeness, and he is back in ministry today. Still, given his history, and with all humility, he is very slow to opt into situations where he might be alone with a female colleague. Simply put, my friend knows himself and is aware of his gender brokenness, and that self-knowledge rightly influences the decisions he makes in mixed-gender partnership situations.

Second, increased self-awareness often results in greater inner healing. Generally speaking, as we more fully understand ourselves, we become better able to move toward wholeness. This reality is confirmed in David's story. Confronted with his unexamined gender brokenness, David turns to the Lord in repentance and confession, and in that experience he finds both greater self-awareness and wholeness, resulting in renewed praise and worship. We see this in Psalm 51, where David exclaims,

> My tongue will sing aloud of your deliverance.
> O Lord, open my lips,
> and my mouth will declare your praise.

In her book *Strengthening the Soul of Your Leadership*, Ruth Haley Barton makes the case that the most effective leaders are the people who have done their often-painful inner work. In fact, she states that "only those who have faced their own dark side can be trusted to lead others toward the Light."[16] If God's mission is going to advance in our communities through flourishing mixed-gender ministry partnerships, we are going to need women and men who have purposefully engaged their inner worlds, specifically in the area of gender brokenness, and have emerged aware and strengthened for their ministry callings.

Third, an increase in self-awareness equips us to more effectively engage with our ministry partners. In their work on the Enneagram, Ian Cron and Suzanne Stabile capture the integration of self-awareness with proper engagement with others. "The point of [Enneagram work] is self-understanding and growing beyond the self-defeating dimensions of our personality, as well as improving relationships and growing in compassion for others."[17]

---

[16]Ruth Haley Barton, *Strengthening the Soul of Your Leadership: Seeking God in the Crucible of Ministry* (Downers Grove, IL: InterVarsity Press, 2008), 44.

[17]Ian Morgan Cron and Suzanne Stabile, *The Road Back to You: An Enneagram Journey to Self-Discovery* (Downers Grove, IL: InterVarsity Press, 2016), 24. The Enneagram is an ancient tool used to discern a person's primary motivations, organized around nine fundamental types.

Individuals should pursue greater self-awareness for their own sake but also for the sake of those around them, including those of the opposite gender with whom they partner in ministry.

BARRIERS TO INCREASING SELF-AWARENESS

Self-awareness is a critical attribute for people who would aspire to create flourishing mixed-gender ministry partnerships. Unfortunately, there are at least four barriers to developing a healthy sense of self-awareness in the area of gender brokenness. First, it can be difficult to make time to do the introspective work required to develop self-awareness. In his book *The Holy Longing*, Ronald Rolheiser writes,

> It is not that we have anything against God, depth, and spirit, we would like these, it's just that we are habitually too preoccupied to have any of these show up on our radar screens. We are more busy than bad, more distracted than nonspiritual, and more interested in the movie theater, the sports stadium, and the shopping mall and the fantasy life they produce in us than we are in the church. Pathological busyness, distraction, and restlessness are major blocks today within our spiritual lives.[18]

Growing in self-awareness requires purposeful and intentional time and attention, and too often we can struggle to make space for such things.

Second, we live in hypersexualized culture that encourages us to freely partake in all manner of sexual gratification. In this context, if we are not aware of our gender brokenness, we may well find ourselves, like David, making poor choices. For instance, the porn industry is a cultural juggernaut. According to *Psychology Today*, in 2017 one popular pornographic website saw eighty-one million total visits, which amounts to roughly fifty-six thousand per minute. Overall, that site ranked thirty-sixth on the list of most-visited websites, but removing various search engines would move it up to fourth, behind only Netflix, Microsoft, and Wikipedia.[19] And, of course, that site is just one place where people can find and experience pornography on the internet.[20] If we are

---

[18]Ronald Rolheiser, *The Holy Longing: The Search for Christian Spirituality* (New York: Doubleday, 1999), 32-33.

[19]Michael Castleman, "Surprising New Data from the World's Most Popular Porn Site," *Psychology Today*, March 15, 2018, www.psychologytoday.com/us/blog/all-about-sex/201803/surprising -new-data-the-world-s-most-popular-porn-site.

[20]Sadly, the church is not immune to the malady of pornography. For instance, Covenant Eyes estimates that one in five youth pastors and one in seven senior pastors use porn on a regular basis,

not aware of our brokenness, the effect of this omnipresent sexual content can be catastrophic. In her book *Beyond Awkward Side Hugs*, Bronwyn Lea writes, "Our sex-crazed culture trains our minds to see people primarily as sexual beings and/or potential sexual partners, rather than as human beings, potential friends, and ministry partners."[21]

Third, as was mentioned in chapter two, topics related to gender brokenness are often considered taboo in our faith communities. We have so privatized the topic of sex—as something that individuals work out in the context of their own discipleship—that to bring up it in a public setting feels awkward or shameful.

And yet Jesus' example would challenge us in this area. Even in mixed-gender contexts, Jesus was willing to speak to the taboo topics. In chapter two, we examined Jesus' interaction with the woman at the well in John 4, a conversation that included a fairly detailed review of her sexual/marital history. To be sure, individuals and communities should be thoughtful about the details of what and how to share, but overcoming the barrier of silence would be a useful corrective.

A fourth barrier to developing self-awareness around gender brokenness is the cultural expectation to "have it all together." In too many social sectors—including the church—to show anything less than perfection is unacceptable, and so we do everything we can to mask our brokenness. This subtle pressure can hold us back from doing the work of developing self-awareness.

David Benner calls our response to the temptation to present ourselves as perfect the "art of packaging our self." He writes, "We learn that even if we feel afraid, we can appear to be brave. We also learn to cloak hate with apparent love, anger with apparent calm, and indifference with apparent sympathy. In short, we learn how to present our self in the best possible light—a light designed to create a favorable impression and maintain our self-esteem."[22] None of us "have it all together," and yet the felt need to appear as such can prevent us from pursuing greater self-awareness in this area.

These four barriers—the inability to take on the required introspective work, our hypersexualized culture, the off-limits nature of the subject in our

---

and 64 percent of Christian men and 15 percent of Christian women say they watch porn at least once per month. See "Pornography Statistics," www.covenanteyes.com/pornstats/.

[21]Bronwyn Lea, *Beyond Awkward Side Hugs: Living as Christian Brothers and Sisters in a Sex-Crazed World* (Nashville: Thomas Nelson, 2020), 11.

[22]David G. Benner, *The Gift of Being Yourself: The Sacred Call to Self-Discovery* (Downers Grove, IL: InterVarsity Press, 2004), 78.

churches, and the cultural expectation to have it all together—can get in the way of our pursuit of self-awareness in the area of gender brokenness.

How to Develop Self-Awareness of Gender Brokenness

Growing in this attribute of self-awareness around gender brokenness starts with honest introspection. We must intentionally make space to reflect on and face our brokenness. Recently, I was presenting on this material with a group of leaders, and one man asked me for a template question that could be used to access issues of gender brokenness in our lives. In response, we worked together to articulate the following question: *How is my gendered identity flawed and in need of redemption, and how is my view of the other gender flawed and in need of redemption?* Honestly reflecting on this question before the Lord would be a great place to start during times of solitude, and then sharing with trusted friends would be a worthwhile next step.

Second, our faith communities can and should catalyze a person's discipleship around gender brokenness. Self-awareness and wholeness in this area can start with intentional disciple-making.

As mentioned in the introduction, I was mentored in college by an InterVarsity staff worker named Úna. I learned so much from Úna during my time under her care; she taught me how to be a leader, how to truly experience Christian community, and how to share my faith. She also took my formation seriously. She wanted me to be more like Jesus and was willing to ask me the hard questions to get me there. It was uncomfortable for me when Úna asked me about my issues with gender brokenness, but I am so grateful that she did because God used her leadership in my life to increase my self-awareness and to start me on the road toward greater wholeness in this area.[23]

Third, individuals and communities—and especially leaders in those communities—should make space to talk about gender brokenness. Just because topics under the umbrella of gender brokenness have historically been taboo doesn't mean they need to stay that way. Creating safe spaces to talk about these things in both single and mixed-gender settings will serve to

---

[23]The simple fact that this mentoring relationship was mixed-gender was significant as well. For one thing, it created for me an interest in this topic, one that obviously continues today. For another, there was something powerful about confessing my gender brokenness to a woman. To have Úna, as a woman, impart forgiveness in this area was a transformative experience for me.

normalize these conversations.[24] Over time, these conversations should get easier and deeper.

In her book *Real Sex*, Lauren Winner offers a vision for communal discipleship around sex and sexuality. She writes,

> The Bible tells us to intrude—or rather, the Bible tells us that talking to one another about what is really going on in our lives is in fact not an intrusion at all, because what's going on in my life is already your concern; by dint of baptism that made me your sister, my joys are your joys and my crises are your crises. We are called to speak to one another lovingly, to be sure, and with edifying, rather than gossipy or hurtful, goals. But we are called nonetheless to transform seemingly private matters into communal matters.[25]

Making room to talk about gender brokenness in a safe environment should give people permission to pursue greater self-awareness in the context of community.

FINAL THOUGHTS

One thing hasn't changed in the two millennia since the ancient Greeks chiseled the words "know thyself" on the wall of their temple: the reality that accruing self-awareness can be hard work. Benjamin Franklin, noted American inventor and statesman, captured this idea well: "There are three Things extremely hard, Steel, a Diamond and to know one's self."[26]

It takes intentionality and diligence to fully examine one's "hidden heart." And then it takes even more effort to do the work to mitigate gender brokenness and to move ahead toward wholeness. The good news is that as that happens, individuals will become better equipped to create mixed-gender ministry partnerships that are personally satisfying and missionally effective.

PROCESSING QUESTIONS

1. What adjective would you use to describe your level of self-awareness in the area of gender brokenness? Why that adjective?

---

[24]I hope that one of the lasting effects of the #MeToo and #ChurchToo era is an ability to talk about topics that have historically been difficult for communities to discuss. See chap. 9 for more about #MeToo and #ChurchToo in the context of mixed-gender communication.

[25]Lauren F. Winner, *Real Sex: The Naked Truth About Chastity* (Grand Rapids, MI: Brazos, 2005), 53.

[26]Benjamin Franklin, *Autobiography: Poor Richard, Letters* (New York: Appleton, 1904), 195.

2. What keeps you from being more self-aware in this area? How could you overcome your barriers?

3. Use this introspective question to discern where you can grow and develop in self-awareness: How is my gendered identity flawed and in need of redemption, and how is my view of the other gender flawed and in need of redemption?

4. What is one thing you could do this week to grow in this area?

5. Who is someone in your life that you could process these things with?

PART 2

COMMUNITY CULTURE

COMMUNITY CULTURE
▲ Vision for Freely Shared Power
▲ Differences for the Sake of Mission
▲ Value for Holistic Friendships
▲ Corporate Sensitivity to Adverse
Gender Dynamics

PLENTY OF WRITERS HAVE ENGAGED THE TOPIC of community or organizational culture.[1] In the literature, culture has been described as powerful, tricky to identify, and malleable.

S. Chris Edmonds emphasizes the sheer power of culture. To do so, he utilizes the metaphor of an engine, noting that culture "drives everything that happens in an organization each day."[2] Edmonds's metaphor is confirmed by Kathie Sorensen and Curt Coffman in their book *Culture Eats Strategy for Lunch*, where they note that "the world we find ourselves in (our cultural experience) either enhances or diminishes our life, our growth and our contribution."[3]

---

[1] Most of the literature discusses "organizational culture," but in this part of the book I am going to use the term *community culture*, primarily because I want to broaden the context to include churches and other faith communities in addition to more traditional organizational settings.
[2] S. Chris Edmonds, *The Culture Engine: A Framework for Driving Results, Inspiring Your Employees, and Transforming Your Workplace* (Hoboken, NJ: John Wiley & Sons, 2014), xv.
[3] Kathie Sorensen and Curt Coffman, *Culture Eats Strategy for Lunch: The Secret of Extraordinary Results Igniting the Passion Within* (Denver: Liang Addison, 2013), 19. Sorensen and Coffman's title riffs on

Without question, community culture is hugely influential in a person's experience.

Next, in his seminal book on culture, Edgar Schein speaks to the complexity of identifying community culture, noting that culture "is a pattern or system of beliefs, values, and behavioral norms that come to be taken for granted as basic assumptions and eventually drop out of awareness."[4] In Schein's rubric, while there are some cultural artifacts that are evident and obvious, there are others that are more difficult to observe, including unwritten rules of the game, integrating symbols, and mental models. Culture can be tricky to parse.

Finally, in his book *Culture Making*, Andy Crouch argues that culture is something that humans are wired to shape. "Culture is what we make of the world. Culture is, first of all, the name for our relentless, restless human effort to take the world as it's given to us and make something else."[5] Crouch reminds us that though culture is powerful and can be difficult to spot, it can and should be crafted by individuals and communities.

When it comes to mixed-gender ministry partnerships, community culture makes a big impact. When a community's culture encourages or champions mixed-gender ministry partnerships, they are more likely to become personally satisfying and missionally effective. Sadly, the converse is also true, as an inhospitable community culture can stymie flourishing partnerships.

My research revealed four attributes of community cultures that promote flourishing mixed-gender partnerships: a vision for shared power, an appreciation of differences for the sake of advancing the mission, a value for holistic friendships, and a corporate awareness of adverse gender dynamics. When intentional effort is given to planting and nurturing these attributes, mixed-gender ministry partnerships can flourish in greater measure.

---

a quip attributed to iconic management consultant Peter Drucker, who supposedly commented that "culture eats strategy for breakfast."

[4]Edgar H. Schein, *Organizational Culture and Leadership*, 5th ed. (Hoboken, NJ: John Wiley & Sons, 2017), 6.

[5]Andy Crouch, *Culture Making: Recovering Our Creative Calling* (Downers Grove, IL: InterVarsity Press, 2008), 23.

5

VISION FOR FREELY SHARED POWER

AMONG OTHER THINGS, QUALITATIVE RESEARCHERS are concerned with obtaining valid data.[1] One way to do this is to utilize multiple research approaches—the theory being that if diverse methodologies produce similar results, the data are more likely to be considered valid. Accordingly, I deployed three research methods in my study: semi-structured interviews, focus-group interviews, and participant-observation studies.

Each of the three methodologies produced solid (and ultimately valid) data, and each was enjoyable, but my favorite approach was the observational one. In a participant-observation study, the researcher joins a group in a meeting or event, looking for data that can answer their research questions. In my case, I conducted two such studies, where I joined regularly scheduled InterVarsity staff meetings, paying attention to the gender dynamics in the room. In both cases, it was a joy to personally see and feel the dynamics, as opposed to simply hearing someone talk about them in an interview setting.

In one of the studies, a group of leaders had gathered for a day-long meeting with a primary focus on evangelism strategy. There were twelve people in the room, and while I was interested in all gender dynamics, I was paying particular attention to the woman and man who were coleading the meeting. I was curious about how they would share the leadership role and how they would choose to present themselves to their team.

While they did several things that portrayed a vibrant and equitable partnership, including alternating leadership through the day, one subtle aspect of their leadership stood out to me like a flashing light. When one of the leaders would be up front leading, they would invariably verbally represent the other.

---

[1] Validity "refers to the accuracy and trustworthiness of instruments, data, and findings in research. Nothing in research is more important than validity." H. Russell Bernard, *Research Methods in Anthropology: Qualitative and Quantitative Approaches*, 5th ed. (Lanham, MD: AltaMira, 2011), 41-42.

For example, when someone on their team asked a question that would re-quire further consideration, the response was, "Let [my partner] and me talk, and we'll get back to you on that."[2]

A phrase like this was uttered probably twenty times over the course of the day, and its repeated use drove home an important point—namely, these leaders took power sharing seriously, to the point that if one of their super-visees had talked to one of them, they had essentially talked to the other as well. When communities embrace and exhibit a vision for freely shared power, they are more likely to be populated by flourishing mixed-gender ministry partnerships.

POWER: AN OVERVIEW

Before discussing the idea of freely shared power in the Scriptures and in the research, it will be helpful to take a brief look at the notion of power—its defi-nition, where it comes from in a community, and how it develops in a person.

First, in his book *Playing God*, Andy Crouch defines power as "the ability to make something of the world."[3] Crouch notes that power has its origins in the Genesis account and that "power is for flourishing. This means power is a gift worth asking for, seeking and—should we receive it—stewarding."[4] This optimistic vision of power is inspiring, but of course power can also be used to cause pain and destruction. In *Making Room for Leadership*, MaryKate Morse brings helpful clarity to the use of power: "Though power itself is neutral, how we use it is not. Power can be used for good or bad. Power can water a garden or flood a valley."[5]

Next, in an organizational or communal setting, power can come from a variety of sources. In *Reframing Organizations*, Bolman and Deal cite nine dif-ferent sources of power. For instance, people can operate using positional power. Professors, pastors, and organizational managers tend to wield

---

[2]This example not only captures the spirit of this chapter, a "vision for freely shared power," but it also illustrates the importance of identifying and mitigating adverse gender dynamics (see chap. 8) as well as a value for public affirmation and modeling (see chap. 11).

[3]Andy Crouch, *Playing God: Redeeming the Gift of Power* (Downers Grove, IL: InterVarsity Press, 2013), 17. Crouch is approaching the concept of power from a biblical or Christian perspective, but it is worth noting that his definition of power resonates with secular definitions of power. For instance, Lee G. Bolman and Terrence E. Deal define power as "the capacity to make things happen." *Refram-ing Organizations: Artistry, Choice, and Leadership*, 4th ed. (San Francisco: John Wiley & Sons, 2008), 196.

[4]Crouch, *Playing God*, 37.

[5]MaryKate Morse, *Making Room for Leadership: Power, Space and Influence* (Downers Grove, IL: Inter-Varsity Press, 2008), 43.

positional power. Another source of power is personal power, where a person's charisma or social skills drive their ability to make something of the world. Other sources of power include control of rewards, coercion, information and expertise, reputation, alliances and networks, access and control of agendas, and control of meaning and symbols.[6] Understanding where power comes from can be important in discerning how to wield it effectively.

Finally, Janet Hagberg notes that power is something that can be developed or cultivated in a person over time. In her book *Real Power*, Hagberg lays out six stages of power. Stage one is powerlessness, and then in stage two people gain power through association. That is, they have power because of their proximity to other people with more power. In stage three, power comes by achievement. People with titles and positions tend to be at stage three, "the most common stage in organizations."[7] Stage-four power is power by reflection, where a person begins to embrace their internal sense of agency, but stage four is often followed by an internal wall, where a person's self-concept gets challenged. If they can successfully navigate the wall, people can progress to the final two stages of Hagberg's model, power by purpose and power by wisdom.

All in all, social power, the ability to make something of the world, is a gift from God that needs to be stewarded with care. Beyond that, power can come from many different places, and it is something that can be developed. When communities can discern ways to equitably share power, women and men are more likely to experience mixed-gender ministry partnerships that are personally satisfying and missionally effective.

SHARING POWER IN SCRIPTURE

A vision for freely shared power has its origins in the first pages of the Bible. As mentioned in the introduction to this book, the first chapter of Genesis lays out God's vision for how power is meant to work in a mixed-gender ministry partnership, and one of the main ideas is that power should be freely shared.

Again, in Genesis 1:28 we read, "God blessed them, and God said to them, 'Be fruitful and multiply, and fill the earth and subdue it; and have dominion over the fish of the sea and over the birds of the air and over every living thing that moves upon the earth.'" This universal mandate makes clear God's intention

---

[6]Bolman and Deal, *Reframing Organizations*, 203-4.
[7]Janet O. Hagberg, *Real Power: Stages of Personal Power in Organizations*, 3rd ed. (Salem, WI: Sheffield, 2003), xv. Tragically but interestingly, Hagberg notes that "most of our American organizational culture is at stage three" (xxiii).

for the full and equal partnership between women and men in the ministry context. Together they were to fill the earth, together they were to subdue it, and together they would exercise dominion. Freely shared power has been God's design for mixed-gender ministry partnerships since the very beginning.

Perhaps the best biblical example of power sharing in the context of a mixed-gender ministry partnership is that of the married couple Priscilla and Aquila. These partners make six appearances in the New Testament narrative, and what is intriguing is that Priscilla's name comes first four of those times, while on two occasions Aquila's name leads the way.[8]

The first mention of these two leaders comes in Acts 18:2, where we meet Aquila and then Priscilla, and where we learn that they are refugees in Corinth, having had to flee Rome because of their Jewish heritage. Later, in Acts 18:18, Priscilla and Aquila sail with Paul to Ephesus, where they were left to care for the church there. Next, during their time in Ephesus, they correct the theology of a leader named Apollos, and the text is careful to note in Acts 18:24-28 that Apollos was challenged by Priscilla and Aquila.[9]

The ministry couple makes three appearances in the Epistles as well. In Romans 16:3, Paul acknowledges his partners Prisca and Aquila.[10] Then in 1 Corinthians 16:19, Aquila is named first as Paul cites the couple's role as house-church leaders. Finally, Prisca and Aquila are once again mentioned in the closing greetings in 2 Timothy 4:19.

What should we make of the constant flipping of the order of their names? One theory holds that in a situation like this one, the person named first "belonged to a higher social status and was more prominent and knowledgeable."[11] If that is true, by alternating the order of Priscilla and Aquila's names, the New

---

[8]Craig Keener notes how irregular it was for a wife to have her name listed first. "That Priscilla's name is mentioned before her husband's in Romans 16:3 and twice in Acts is noteworthy, because the husband was nearly always mentioned first unless the wife was of higher social status or neither party had any concern for status." *Paul, Women, & Wives: Marriage and Women's Ministry in the Letters of Paul* (Peabody, MA: Hendrickson, 1992), 241.

[9]In *Man and Woman, One in Christ: An Exegetical and Theological Study of Paul's Letters* (Grand Rapids, MI: Zondervan, 2009), Philip B. Payne notes the significance of Priscilla having influence over Apollos's theology: "Since Scripture speaks with approval of a woman instructing [Apollos], it is hard to imagine any man who would be above being taught by a woman or any theological topic that would be out of bounds for a woman" (64).

[10]Craig Keener notes that "Prisca" is the Latin diminutive form of "Priscilla." *The IVP Bible Background Commentary: New Testament* (Downers Grove, IL: InterVarsity Press, 1993), 447.

[11]Susan Mathew, *Women in the Greetings of Romans 16.1-16: A Study of Mutuality and Women's Ministry in the Letter to the Romans* (New York: Bloomsbury Academic, 2013), 88. In general, scholars agree that there is significance in the name order in situations like this one. For instance, John McRay notes that the person named first has "higher status." *Paul: His Life and Teaching* (Grand Rapids, MI: Baker Academic, 2003), 169.

Testament writers could well have been putting the emphasis on the inter-changeability of their ministry together. In some situations Aquila was "more prominent and knowledgeable"; other times Priscilla was.[12] In this way, there was a fluidity of leadership in their mixed-gender ministry partnership. They really and truly shared power.

To be sure, this couple had a robust and vital ministry: partnering with Paul, pastoring the churches in Ephesus and Corinth, correcting the theology of ascendant leaders, and more. Given the choices that the ancient writers made interchanging their names, it appears that this mixed-gender ministry part-nership also featured the free sharing of power.

FREELY SHARED POWER IN THE RESEARCH

In alignment with God's Genesis vision for shared power as well as the biblical example of Priscilla and Aquila, research participants repeatedly voiced the importance of freely shared power as they reflected on core attributes of flour-ishing mixed-gender ministry partnerships. In fact, this attribute was the most frequently mentioned component in the research. In talking about this vision for shared power, participants spoke of "a sense of real equality around the table" and an experience where "everyone is invited to speak and all voices are heard."

To be sure, there is a countercultural element to this vision of freely shared power. In short, the world doesn't tend to view power in these ways. In one interview, a woman was talking about this notion of shared power, and in doing so she held her hands out in front of her with her palms up. It struck me as an important visual, to be openhanded about power. By contrast, too often the world's paradigm of power is embodied by a clenched fist.[13]

This vision for shared power was particularly countercultural for several of the male participants in the study. One man captured this reality by describing his intentional efforts to follow the leadership of his female supervisor. Noting

---

[12]Linda Belleville, "Women Leaders in the Bible," in *Discovering Biblical Equality: Complementarity Without Hierarchy*, ed. Ronald W. Pierce and Rebecca Merrill Groothuis (Downers Grove, IL: Inter-Varsity Press, 2004), argues that the changing order reflects distinct roles or responsibilities: "When New Testament writers refer to their occupation of tentmakers and to 'their house,' the order is 'Aquila and Priscilla.' But when ministry is in view, the order is 'Priscilla and Aquila'" (122).

[13]Plenty of thinkers have explored the seductive allure of power. For instance, Richard Foster writes, "For us, it is never enough to enjoy good work. No, we must obtain supremacy; we must possess; we must hoard; we must conquer. The sin of power is the yearning to be more than we are created to be. We want to be gods." *Money, Sex, and Power: The Challenge of the Disciplined Life* (San Francisco: Harper & Row, 1985), 175.

his "absolute commitment to not jockeying for position," this man expressed his posture in this way: "It is your call. I will chime in, but I will follow your lead." In another interview, a man described his habit of reflection on the question, "Am I willing to abdicate power?"[14]

Pragmatically, respondents offered several examples for what the manifestation of this vision for freely shared power might entail, and the repeated emphasis was on reciprocity. That is, flourishing is more likely to happen when women and men are looking for ways to empower and advocate for one another. For instance, one female supervisor told a story about how she had been blessed by her male ministry partner's advocacy, stating, "I would not be the person I am today if it were not for his work and his sponsorship." Likewise, a male leader remarked how important his female ministry partner's influence had been for him, both in his life as a disciple and in his organizational leadership.

Given that this vision for freely shared power tends to be countercultural, many interviewees noted the importance of intentionally setting up reciprocal partnerships. One long-serving leader shared her observation that "the strongest male/female partnerships I've seen in InterVarsity . . . are super intentional about discussing rights, responsibilities, parameters, and expectations."[15] Similarly, a male respondent remarked, "I think we've got to talk about power. We get tripped up when we don't talk about it."

The bottom line is that most people surveyed for this project were craving a countercultural experience regarding power with respect to gender. Moving beyond a clenched-fist notion of power, they are eager to articulate and live out a vision for freely shared, open-handed power in their mixed-gender interactions with one another.

BENEFITS OF FREELY SHARED POWER

Embracing and embodying a vision for freely shared power in the context of mixed-gender ministry partnerships should result in several specific benefits.

---

[14]As alluded to in some of the quotes in this chapter, the journey to an incarnated vision for freely shared power will be different for women and men. For women, who have too often been pushed to the margins, this journey could include learning to see power as a positive thing and gaining a vision for how to wield it well. For men, the journey could include acknowledging that they have historically held the majority of power in so many cultural contexts and then releasing power in order for women to thrive. For several years, I chronicled my personal journey of engaging the intersection of power, faith in Jesus, and my male gender at challengingtertullian.com. See also Wilmer Villacorta, *Unmasking the Male Soul: Power and Gender Trap for Women in Leadership* (Eugene, OR: Wipf & Stock, 2019).

[15]This statement also illustrates the importance of abundant communication (see chap. 9).

First, sharing power can allow for the division of ministry tasks by giftings, passions, and callings. A vision for freely shared power can allow the community to determine ministry assignments based on how someone is wired, without the usual gender-based constraints. Utilizing tools such as spiritual gifts inventories, the Enneagram, and the CliftonStrengths assessment can help communities determine where a particular individual might fit strategically in the ministry context.[16]

I have a friend who served for many years as a solo pastor of a small congregation. Because he was a solo pastor, he was by necessity a jack-of-all-trades. In any given moment, he could be preparing the Sunday sermon, counseling a struggling parishioner, working on the church budget, or climbing in the church attic working on the building's air-conditioning system. It was overwhelming for him to take on all those roles, and my observation was that he was too often operating outside of his giftings and passions. Most notably, the Sunday sermon requirement prohibited him from doing what I think he is particularly wired to do, pastoring people in crisis. Consistently operating outside of his giftings took a toll, and he eventually left the pastorate. Thankfully, he found a job in the chaplaincy field, and now he operates almost exclusively within his gift mix.

There is no easy fix for someone in my friend's situation, but a vision for shared power offers one possible solution. If my friend could have assembled a diverse lay leadership team, it could have benefited everyone. Not only would it have lightened his personal workload, but the congregation could benefit from the varied giftings of people on the team. In addition, each person would benefit from space to develop in her/his particular gifts.

A second benefit of embracing a vision for freely shared power is that more people can be given a voice. This can be particularly significant for women, who too often have their voices silenced. In a community culture marked by an open-handed vision for power, more people can have more access to both the agenda and the microphone. In her book *Raise Your Voice*, Kathy Khang writes, "Our voice—our influence and interaction with people and the world around us—is embodied through our words and actions. When we understand our

---

[16]For more on the Enneagram, see Ian Morgan Cron and Suzanne Stabile, *The Road Back to You: An Enneagram Journey to Self-Discovery* (Downers Grove, IL: InterVarsity Press, 2016). The Clifton-Strengths Assessment helps individuals understand how they are uniquely wired, so that they can then turn their natural talents into strengths; see www.gallup.com/cliftonstrengths/en/252137/home.aspx. For more on discerning how someone is uniquely wired for service, see chap. 6.

voice, we echo God's character and good news. . . . Our voice is both word and deed."[17] A lived-out vision for freely shared power can increase capacity for women as well as men to exercise their God-given voices. As that happens, we should expect our missional effectiveness to increase.

A third benefit of embracing a vision for freely shared power borrows from the principle of checks and balances. Having colleagues in partnership sharing power can provide built-in feedback and accountability. In my partnership with my colleague Layla, we constantly check one another by offering honest feedback. It can feel vulnerable to put my ideas forward for critique, but the trust I have with Layla mitigates that dynamic. Her input consistently makes my thinking better, and our organization benefits from decisions that have been vetted by our diverse perspectives.

Finally, adopting a shared power type of arrangement at a leadership level can open up more access for followers. The job-sharing ministry partnership described in the beginning of this chapter afforded followers a chance to interact with either of the two leaders, which increased their points of contact with the organizational levels above them, and it allowed them to interact with a diversity of leadership.

BARRIERS TO FREELY SHARED POWER

As the research demonstrates, when communities adopt and embody a vision for freely shared power, mixed-gender ministry partnerships are more likely to flourish. Sadly, there are two particular barriers that can prevent communities from adopting this vision and practice.

To begin with, too many of our churches and organizations have simply borrowed their view of power from the world's perspective. Having a clenched-fist vision of power will obviously make it difficult to adopt a philosophy of freely shared power.[18]

In 2017, five pastors wrote an article for *Christianity Today* titled "We Were Seduced by Power."[19] In the piece, the pastors noted their battles with four

---

[17]Kathy Khang, *Raise Your Voice: Why We Stay Silent and How to Speak Up* (Downers Grove, IL: InterVarsity Press, 2018), 36.

[18]How a community's vision of power gets formed is surely a complex process. The world's view of power factors into this process, but there are other factors as well, including a community's theological understanding and ethnic/cultural background.

[19]Jamin Goggin, Glenn Packiam, J. R. Briggs, Joshua Ryan Butler, and Tyler Johnson, "We Were Seduced by Power," *Christianity Today,* January 30, 2017, www.christianitytoday.com/pastors/2017/january-web-exclusives/we-were-seduced-by-power.html.

different types of temptations: the power to manipulate, the power to be significant, the power to make a name for themselves, and the power to control. They wrote, "Pastors are in a position of power. Our vocation is vested with influence. If we remain naïve or stubbornly inattentive to this reality, we will fall prey to worldly forms of power in ministry. We need to cultivate honest dialogue marked by repentance and exhortation. In short, we need to confess to one another." The church's uncritical embrace of the world's thinking regarding power means that shared power partnerships tend to be infrequent, and that is particularly true for mixed-gender ministry partnerships.

A second barrier to communities embracing a vision for shared power is the prevailing model of solitary leadership. In essentially every sector of society, the default leadership setting is power consolidated in one particular person.[20] Today's conventional wisdom dictates that there can only be one general, one CEO, one president, and one pastor. And while none of these leaders functions completely in a vacuum, the reality is that the power structure flows to—and from—that single individual.

In contrast to this prevailing view, recent scholarship has affirmed the viability of shared power forms of leadership in a variety of spaces. Writing in *Harvard Business Review*, executive coach Marshall Goldsmith notes that "shared leadership involves maximizing all of the human resources in an organization by empowering individuals and giving them an opportunity to take leadership positions in their areas of expertise. With more complex markets increasing the demands on leadership, the job in many cases is simply too large for one individual."[21]

Similarly, writing from a faith-based perspective, Danielle Strickland notes, "Not only is this original design [of shared leadership] the answer for women who feel limited and stuck and outside of the leadership zone. It's also the answer for men who feel lonely, overworked, exhausted, and stuck on the wheel of production and provision. God's original best-case design is for a

---

[20]And, predictably, that person is almost always a man. A 2018 *New York Times* article described the results of a simple survey conducted by organizational psychologists, where they asked people to draw a picture of a "leader." "In terms of gender, the results are almost always the same. Both men and women almost always draw men. 'Even when the drawings are gender neutral,' which is uncommon, Dr. Kiefer said in an email, 'the majority of groups present the drawing using language that indicates male (he) rather than neutral or female.'" Heather Murphy, "Picture a Leader. Is She a Woman?," *New York Times*, March 16, 2018, www.nytimes.com/2018/03/16/health/women -leadership-workplace.html.

[21]Marshall Goldsmith, "Sharing Leadership to Maximize Talent," *Harvard Business Review*, May 26, 2010, https://hbr.org/2010/05/sharing-leadership-to-maximize.

shared leadership structure. A team model. Shared responsibility."[22] If faith communities want to see their mission advance in greater measure, they ought to strongly consider embracing a vision for freely shared power expressed in shared leadership models.

How to Develop and Embody a Vision for Shared Power

There are several practical steps that communities can take to more fully embrace and exemplify a vision and practice of freely shared power. First, communities can create safe spaces to explore their theological perspectives on power. Several years ago, I invited Noemi, one of my ministry partners, to join our executive leadership team. From my perspective, it looked like the perfect move. Noemi had plenty of gifts that we could use on the team, the particular job description we had offered her was a great fit, and relational trust was high with myself as well as with the other people on the team. In addition, she was open to the move, for the same reasons. Still, as we processed the decision, it was clear that she faced a significant theological impediment.

Noemi had spent her entire life experiencing the underside of power. As a Latina from a lower-income background, Noemi had essentially experienced perpetual powerlessness. Since she had lived almost exclusively on the margins, she had developed a negative view of power, and because of that she was hesitant to join a team that wielded the majority of the organizational power in our ministry context.

In the end, Noemi joined our team and made wonderful contributions. What made that possible was an intensive season of theological reflection. Specifically, Noemi spent around six months studying the Gospels, exclusively examining Jesus' use of power. It was a revolutionary study, one which opened the door to her embracing a vision for freely shared power.[23]

One of the action steps from chapter three above involved an exhortation to create safe spaces for individuals and communities to explore their theologies around gender equality. Likewise, following Noemi's example into focused theological reflection on power would be a worthwhile endeavor for

---

[22]Danielle Strickland, *Better Together: How Women and Men Can Heal the Divide and Work Together to Transform the Future* (Nashville: Thomas Nelson, 2020), 143.

[23]Since this experience, Noemi has cowritten a book on Latina identity and leadership titled *Hermanas*. The entire book is wonderful, and Noemi's chapters on the bleeding woman, Rahab, Tabitha, and Mary include her views on power in a Latina context. Natalia Kohn, Noemi Vega Quiñones, and Kristy Garza Robinson, *Hermanas: Deepening Our Identity and Growing our Influence* (Downers Grove, IL: InterVarsity Press, 2019).

communities who wish to promote flourishing mixed-gender ministry partnerships, as well as diversity more broadly.

A second action step that communities can take is to perform a power audit. That is, communities can set aside time to carefully discern how power works in their midst: who has power and who doesn't, and why individuals have power or not. Making space for an unflinching evaluation of how power works can provide data that a community can use in order to proactively allocate, or reallocate, power.

To perform such an audit, communities can utilize MaryKate Morse's framework on power and space. In *Making Room for Leadership*, Morse uses the idea of social space as a metaphor for how much power someone possesses. In Morse's rubric, the more powerful take up more space and the less powerful take up less space. Further, how much space someone takes up is an amalgamation of various social factors. Social factors that take up more space (and thus connote more power) include being a man, being white, making more money, being older, being taller, being more educated, being married, being charismatic, and others.[24]

Just after Morse's book came out, my leadership team read the book together, and when we were finished, we did a power audit. As a part of that process, we discussed how much space individuals took up on our team. One verdict was unanimous: by virtue of my title, my experience, my age, my gender, my ethnicity, my temperament, and probably ten other social metrics, I took up the most space on our team. I had the most power by far. By contrast, others took up varying lesser degrees of power. Having this power audit conversation was instructive for us, and it allowed us to consider how we might redistribute the power on our team. For instance, in response, we developed a plan where I would delegate leadership of various topics during our team meetings, thus decreasing the amount of space I took up and growing the influence of others, including Noemi, in our leadership community.[25]

Third, organizational leaders can extend permission for people to experiment with shared leadership models. They can appoint coleaders for an

---

[24]MaryKate Morse, *Making Room for Leadership: Power, Space and Influence* (Downers Grove, IL: InterVarsity Press, 2008). Morse delineates between visual and visceral marks of social presence. See her story in chap. 8.

[25]This process was not without some level of dissonance for me. I recall processing feelings of shame at taking up so much space, and delegating leadership to others took some effort on my part. Still, the fruit of the reallocation process was profound for all concerned, including myself. Not only did my workload lighten, I found joy in sitting under the leadership of my colleagues.

upcoming project. They can assign a mixed-gender preaching team. They can rotate leadership among members of a ministry team. Creating a laboratory where people can experiment with shared leadership models can provide useful feedback for a community interested in living out a vision for freely shared power. It can also allow individuals to progress more quickly through Hagberg's six stages of power.

Finally, power will only be successfully shared if there is clarity about who is responsible for what. Without clear job descriptions, things can fall through the cracks. This matters in every shared-power scenario, but it is particularly important when people are sharing job roles.

Several years ago, I supervised a couple who job-shared as ministry leaders, a modern-day Priscilla and Aquila. Because of the complexity of the role, we were careful to detail exactly who was responsible for what. And because the job involved supervising a leadership team, we had to let the team know which of the pair they should go to for primary leadership support in a particular situation.[26] While it took work to clarify how the system would operate, the effort proved worthwhile, as the team benefited from their shared leadership.

FINAL THOUGHTS

Given the dominance of the world's clenched-fist view of power, mixed-gender ministry partnerships where this value for freely shared power is faithfully and repeatedly incarnated won't just happen on their own. Instead, building reciprocally empowering partnerships will require energy and effort. They will also require the others-mindedness that emerged clearly in my study.

In one interview, a female supervisor, a leader who had partnered closely in ministry with one particular male colleague for decades, joyfully recalled their collaboration, saying, "He's been an advocate for me, and I've been an advocate for him." Further, she captured the core of this attribute concisely when she told me that their posture has always been "I'm in for you succeeding." It is easy to imagine that Adam and Eve, along with Priscilla and Aquila (or Aquila and Priscilla!), would heartily endorse that posture.

---

[26]We had to take several other steps to make the scenario viable for all concerned. For one thing, as the supervisor I had to view the arrangement as if I were supervising three people, each person in the couple and then the couple as a whole. For another, we created systems to ensure that their working partnership didn't consume their marriage. To help with this, they established standing meetings during the week, with the idea that they would avoid discussing work outside of those designated meeting slots.

PROCESSING QUESTIONS

1. If there is a continuum with a clenched fist on one side and open palms on the other, where do you and your community stand regarding power?

2. What could it look like for you or your community to reimagine your theology of power? How can you begin having conversations about how power works in your community?

3. Conduct a power audit. Who has power in your community and why do they have it? How can or should social power be reconfigured in your context?

4. What is one thing you can do to freely share power with a mixed-gender ministry partner in your context?

6

DIFFERENCES FOR THE SAKE
OF MISSION

As an InterVarsity middle manager, part of my job is conducting transition interviews when employees leave the organization. These exit interviews are always bittersweet, as they create space for people to simultaneously reflect on the wonderful things that God has done in and through them, as well as on the more difficult things they have experienced during their time in the ministry.

Several years ago, I sat with a woman who was leaving after a long and fruitful season of ministry. She had been with InterVarsity for more than twenty years. We walked through the litany of interview questions, and then I asked her about any dissonance she was feeling as she looked back on her years in ministry with InterVarsity.

She sat with my question for several beats, and then she began to softly weep. I encouraged her to take her time and offered her a tissue. After a short while, she looked up at me and said, "I wish I had been given more room to lead as a woman."

When individuals are empowered to lead in ways that are true or authentic to who they are, mixed-gender ministry partnerships are more likely to flourish. For this to happen on a consistent basis, the community culture must endorse the notion that difference is useful for the advancement of our mission. Further, that endorsement should apply whether or not a particular individual adheres to established gender stereotypes.

DIFFERENCES FOR THE SAKE OF MISSION IN THE RESEARCH

Those interviewed for this study affirmed the notion that difference matters in the context of mission. Specifically, the threefold consensus was that differences are real, that they should be welcomed and utilized for the expansion of

God's mission, and that each individual should be empowered to be who they are, whether or not who they are aligns with the dominant gender stereotype.

To begin with, though participants were largely agnostic about where gender differences came from or even what they look like, they were aware of their presence.[1] One male leader summarized the larger pool of input when he said, "Even though I think women are equal to men, I also think they are different. To say 'men, women, doesn't matter'—I don't agree with that."

Next, once differences are recognized, the consensus is that they should be welcomed and deployed for the purpose of advancing our mission. One respondent joyfully recalled how different she and her male ministry partner were during their time partnering together in leadership, noting that "our team got the best of both of us." Another participant captured the practical realities of working together as a mixed-gender team when he talked about their decision that he would take the lead in doing their assigned fundraising asks in the conservative town where they served, on the assumption that he would be better received than his female partner. And another interviewee said, "I think that if you lean into how men and women, generally speaking, tend to bring different instincts, different perspectives, different gifts and leanings, not in any kind of predefined way, then the partnership becomes even more powerful."

So, for those surveyed, differences are something to be recognized and leveraged to advance the mission. But one other significant finding emerged from the research—namely, while interviewees acknowledged the presence of gender stereotypes, they don't think individuals or communities should be beholden to them. That is, individuals should be empowered to be who they are, whether that aligns with the established gender stereotype or not.

In one case, a female leader lamented the hurtful messages she had internalized early on in her ministry career, that women can only lead in prescribed ways. Reflecting on her journey, she used the word *traumatizing* to describe how it felt not fitting the style of leadership that had been established for her gender. Similarly, another respondent said, "I think one of the struggles in

---

[1]The question of gender differences, and specifically the role of nature vs. nurture in the formation of gender differences, has been vigorously debated in the literature. Instead of resolving the debate, I will defer to Mary Stewart Van Leeuwen's three points regarding gender difference: "first, that men and women are more alike than different, both biologically and psychologically; second, that although biology sets limits on what learning can accomplish, learning also affects our biology, including its sex-related aspects; and third, that we cannot appeal to any mechanical combination of nature plus nurture as a way to escape responsibility for our behavior, either as women or men." *Gender & Grace: Love, Work, and Parenting in a Changing World* (Downers Grove, IL: InterVarsity Press, 1990), 76.

gender issues is that women have to try to become more like men and sometimes it's better for men to be a little more like women, whatever that looks
like." Finally, a long-serving supervisor captured this idea best when he defined flourishing as "what happens when people feel safe being who they
uniquely are."

In the end, the research process articulated three clear messages about
gender differences. First, differences are real. Second, they should be welcomed
and leveraged to advance our corporate mission. Third, an individual's gifts,
calling, and temperament are useful for ministry whether or not they align
with the socially accepted gender stereotypes.

DIFFERENCES FOR THE SAKE OF MISSION IN THE SCRIPTURES

These three messages find affirmation in the Scriptures, where difference is
likewise affirmed as vital to God's mission, regardless of whether it overlaps
with the conventional stereotypes or not. On one hand, there are plenty of
women and men in the Bible who present in ways that adhere to the notions
of femininity and masculinity prevalent in the biblical era. For example, in
alignment with the dominant social construct of the day, throughout the Scriptures men tend to operate in the public sphere while women toil in their homes.[2]

On the other hand, there are women and men who tread all over the established gender stereotypes of their day. The Old Testament judge and proph-
etess Deborah is one example. In Judges 4–5 we meet this woman who was a
prophet, a judge, a military leader, and "the commanding force behind Israel's
deliverance."[3] Each of these roles would have been traditionally masculine
ones.[4] And while empathy and emotions were (and continue to be) generally regarded as feminine traits, the prophet Jeremiah is just one of many
men in the Bible who are caught weeping, for various reasons.[5] Jeremiah

---

[2]For a fuller discussion of separate spheres for women and men, see chap. 8's examination of Paul
and Phoebe's mixed-gender ministry partnership.
[3]Arthur E. Cundall and Leon Morris, *Judges & Ruth: An Introduction and Commentary*, Tyndale Old
Testament Commentaries (Downers Grove, IL: InterVarsity Press, 1968), 85.
[4]At one point, when the nation comes under threat from Sisera's army, Israel's military chief, a man
named Barak, balks at Deborah's prophetic command, causing her to issue this judgment: "The road
on which you are going will not lead to your glory, for the LORD will sell Sisera into the hand of a
woman" (Judges 4:9). That woman turns out to be a Kenite woman named Jael, who ultimately
drives a tent peg into a sleeping Sisera's temple, killing him. Needless to say, this would be yet another example of a woman exhibiting behavior that can hardly be labeled "ladylike."
[5]As the so-called weeping prophet, Jeremiah is in some distinguished masculine empathetic company. Other biblical men who cry include Nehemiah (Nehemiah 1:4), David (2 Samuel 15:30),
Timothy (2 Timothy 1:4), and, of course, Jesus (John 11:35).

"broods over his lot in life and wishes that he had never been born, complaining that, though he has lived an upright life, everyone curses him."[6] Even though Deborah and Jeremiah didn't neatly fit the established gender stereotypes of their day, God used them in their uniqueness to advance God's purposes in the world.

Further, the story in Luke 10:38-42 provides evidence that established social gender roles were nonbinding for Jesus. In the text, Jesus is in Martha and Mary's home and it is time to eat. Martha is hard at work with various hosting duties, the socially appropriate role for a woman in her situation. By contrast, her sister Mary is listening to Jesus, sitting at his feet in the position of a disciple. When Martha complains to Jesus, he responds by saying, "Martha, Martha, you are worried and distracted by many things; there is need of only one thing. Mary has chosen the better part, which will not be taken away from her."

From our modern vantage point, it can be difficult to understand how revolutionary Jesus' statement, and its implications, would have been. By lauding Mary's decision, Jesus pointed to learning and intimacy with him as a "higher priority"[7] than the socially appropriate mode of operation for women in his day.[8] Watching Jesus transgress social conventions teaches us that prescribed gender roles and stereotypes should not be an impediment to a person expressing their individuality.

All in all, the Bible affirms the idea that difference is advantageous to God's mission. When individuals are empowered to lead in ways that are authentic for them, the mission moves forward, whether or not someone adheres to the socially accepted gender stereotypes of their day.

BENEFITS OF UTILIZING GENDER DIFFERENCES TO ADVANCE GOD'S MISSION

Faith communities can expect to experience at least two benefits that come from developing a culture that prioritizes individuality over prescribed gender stereotypes. First, there is a substantial body of literature that points out the

---

[6]R. K. Harrison, *Jeremiah & Lamentations: An Introduction & Commentary*, Tyndale Old Testament Commentaries (Downers Grove, IL: InterVarsity Press, 1973), 103.

[7]Catherine Clark Kroeger, "Luke," in *The IVP Women's Bible Commentary*, ed. Catherine Clark Kroeger and Mary J. Evans (Downers Grove, IL: InterVarsity Press, 2002), 575.

[8]In this passage, Mary has clearly made the better choice, but that doesn't mean that Martha didn't make good choices in her life. As Marg Mowczko points out, Martha would later make "some astute statements of faith concerning Jesus' identity and concerning eternal life," in John 11. "Mary, Martha and Lazarus of Bethany," blog, May 15, 2013, https://margmowczko.com/martha-mary-and-lazarus-of-bethany/.

correlation between increased diversity and better bottom-line success. Indeed, much of corporate America has enthusiastically embraced the idea that diversity of gender, race, and other social metrics increases a company's productivity. For example, a 2009 Catalyst study of Fortune 500 companies concluded that those with "sustained representation of women on their boards had 84% better return on sales, 60% better return on invested capital, and 46% higher return on equity."[9]

In part, gender diversity accelerates the mission because of the varied approaches that women and men take in accomplishing a task. Though some of this analysis relies on the concept of gender essentialism, which will be explored later in this chapter, in the last several decades there has been a surge in scholarship about women's contributions in the workplace. For instance, in *The Female Advantage*, Sally Helgesen parses the ways that women tend to work in contrast to men, and she notes that women bring a high value for a healthy balance between people and task into the workplace. She writes, "A picture emerges from the diary studies of women who do not take an instrumental view of either work or people—that is, neither is simply a means to achieving the end of a certain position; both are rather ends in themselves."[10] Similarly, Marie Wilson notes that "the core of what women bring to leadership—a tendency toward greater inclusiveness, empathy, communication up and down hierarchies, focus on broader issues—makes stronger government and richer business."[11]

By and large, the church has not embraced this idea that greater diversity advances mission in the same way that secular America has. Reflecting on the story that began this chapter, what did InterVarsity lose over the twenty years that my staff friend was impeded from leading in ways that were authentic for her? Until women and men are empowered to bring their full and unique selves to the ministry task, mixed-gender partnerships will struggle to flourish in our communities.

Second, when a community culture affirms the perspective that differences are useful for mission, individuals are able to thrive as well. When women and

---

[9]Caroline Turner, *Difference Works: Improving Retention, Productivity, and Profitability Through Inclusion* (Austin, TX: Live Oak, 2012), 12. This is just one of many statistical examples that prove the same point.

[10]Sally Helgesen, *The Female Advantage: Women's Ways of Leadership* (New York: Doubleday, 1990), 29.

[11]Marie Wilson, *Closing the Leadership Gap: Why Women Can and Must Help Run the World* (New York: Viking, 2004), 6.

men are encouraged to lead in ways that are authentic to who they are, there will be greater joy and satisfaction in the work. And as that happens, mixed-gender partnerships should flourish.

As noted previously, it is an understatement to say that my staff partner, Layla, is at her best when she is working with people. She is specifically wired to help people get unstuck when they are struggling. As she and I have partnered together, we have learned the importance of placing her in roles where she can use her strengths. Focusing her role on administration would not place her in a satisfying work situation. Happily, that fits for me. So, in our partnership, we have made decisions that benefit both the bottom line and our personal satisfaction. In the process, our partnership has flourished.

BARRIERS TO UTILIZING GENDER DIFFERENCES TO ADVANCE GOD'S MISSION

Unfortunately, there are at least three barriers to communities embracing and living out this attribute of differences advancing God's mission. If our communities are going to adopt this value, they will need to overcome these potential roadblocks.

The single greatest barrier to embracing the concept of differences benefiting the advancement of our mission are the rigid paradigms that tend to inform our ideas of gender. The concept of gender essentialism asserts that there are immutable gender differences between women and men. For instance, gender essentialism argues that women are wired to be emotional, dedicated, communal, and intuitive. By contrast, men are designed to be driven, analytical, logical, and self-reliant.[12] In the gender essentialist framework, these attributes are locked-in by virtue of one's gender identity.

The biggest problem with gender essentialism is that it pigeonholes women and men into narrow categories, and if a person doesn't fit the paradigm, they are out of luck. Tragically, a lack of fit can have toxic side effects. In 2018, the US National Library of Medicine, a part of the National Institutes of Health, published a study critiquing the notion of gender essentialism. One finding

---

[12]It is not difficult to locate taxonomies that claim to delineate essential masculinity and femininity. For instance, the sample traits referenced here come from pp. 9-10 in *The Athena Doctrine*, a book that makes the intriguing case that "across age, gender, and culture, people around the world feel that feminine traits correlate more strongly with making the world a better place." John Gerzema and Michael D'Antonio, *The Athena Doctrine: How Women (And the Men Who Think Like Them) Will Rule the Future* (San Francisco: Jossey-Bass, 2013), 11.

concluded that "if gender essentialism supports an unequal gender status quo for those who adhere to gender norms and amplifies backlash against women and men who do not adhere to them, then its only real beneficiaries are norm-adhering men."[13]

In her book *Emboldened*, Tara Beth Leach, until recently the senior pastor of First Church of the Nazarene in Pasadena, California, laments her experiences with the shackles that come with a gender-essentialist paradigm:

> It's tempting, then, to try to squeeze myself into some sort of norm that I'll never fit. For example, somewhere deeply ingrained in my psyche is the notion that nurturing and maternal traits are not leadership traits. . . . In fact, there have been plenty who have said that the "feminization of the church" will be the demise of the church—as if feminine traits are negative, weak, and cause for decline. Naturally, then, when I lead with what is sometimes linked to feminine traits, it's a temptation for me to feel doubtful, or worse, shameful.[14]

If mixed-gender ministry partnerships are going to be permitted to flourish, individuals and communities will need to forgo a reliance on gender essentialism. People, created individually in God's image, are unique. In some cases, they will align with the essentialist paradigms, but they will not in others. Women and men will flourish in partnership as communities learn to hold their gender paradigms loosely.

A second barrier is that our default ministry philosophies and structures tend to segregate leadership by gender. In most churches and organizations, men have automatic access to just about any position, from executive leader on down the organizational chart. Put simply, the church has a leadership bias toward men. Women, on the other hand, often have a more limited set of ministry options, and their range of acceptable roles will largely depend on a given faith community's theology of women in leadership.

This ossified system of ecclesiastical gender roles creates two problems. On one hand, men can find themselves in roles for which they are a poor fit. On the other hand, women can find themselves unable to fully express their

---

[13]The bottom-line conclusion in the study was that "psychological research is increasingly revealing the role of gender essentialism in promoting and enabling gender inequality." Lea Skewes, Cordelia Fine, and Nick Haslam, "Beyond Mars and Venus: The Role of Gender Essentialism in Support for Gender Inequality and Backlash," *PLOS ONE* 13, no. 7 (2018): e0200921, doi:10.1371/journal .pone.0200921/.

[14]Tara Beth Leach, *Emboldened: A Vision for Empowering Women in Ministry* (Downers Grove, IL: InterVarsity Press, 2017), 51-52. As Leach goes on to point out, God is described using stereotypically feminine traits in the Scriptures; see, for example, Deuteronomy 32:11; Isaiah 66:13; Hosea 11:3-4.

giftings and callings, limited in their leadership by a so-called "stained-glass ceiling." In *A Woman's Place*, Katelyn Beaty captures the problem that a rigid gender-roles system creates for women:

> In many Christian communities, we slot women into roles—as supporters or helpers, as people who find their identity only through or next to other people. Or we identify women with certain virtues—like gentleness or peace—even though Scripture doesn't dole out the fruits of the Spirit along gender lines (Gal. 5:22). . . . In other words, we make femaleness sound like a to-do list rather than a gift from a mysterious, surprising, and endlessly creative God. This is too bad, because it makes us look more concerned with gender roles than Our Father is.[15]

Our faith communities must move on from this outdated system of gender roles, instead opening up all ministry positions to women as well as men.

A third barrier to a community embracing and living out this value for difference is that discerning and then leveraging differences for the sake of mission can be a time-consuming operation. Discovering who a person is and how they are uniquely wired takes time and attention. It is much easier for a church community to simply install people via a predetermined system of gender roles and expectations.

HOW TO DEVELOP A VALUE FOR DIFFERENCES FOR THE SAKE OF MISSION

In light of these benefits and barriers, how can our communities of faith recognize, welcome, and empower differences for the expansion of our corporate mission? First, faith communities can cultivate a real value for difference, learning to see each person as uniquely called and gifted. Tara Beth Leach notes, "Breaking gender molds, you see, doesn't mean we move from leading one way to another; rather, it means we are free to lead in the only way that we can lead. Be you, dear sister."[16] If our faith communities embrace this perspective, they will see flourishing mixed-gender ministry partnerships develop in greater measure. One tangible way to develop this value for difference would be to digest the literature on this topic. Just because corporate America has a head start on the church in this area doesn't mean it needs to remain that way.

---

[15]Katelyn Beaty, *A Woman's Place: A Christian Vision for Your Calling in the Office, the Home, and the World* (New York: Howard, 2016), 126-27.
[16]Leach, *Emboldened*, 65. These words can and should apply to "brothers" as well.

Second, our communities need to focus on developing people as unique individuals. That process can begin with helping individuals discern how God has specifically wired them and then determining the best places for them to serve in mission. This process might necessitate a reevaluation of a community's leadership development architecture, which may well be designed to develop leaders in a mass-produced style that relies on essentialist norms. Is there room in our hiring, development, and promotion structures and systems for women and men who do not align with the dominant gender stereotypes?

One way to help this to happen is to identify and empower mentors who can effectively do this individualized disciple-making work. "Mentoring is a relational experience through which one person empowers another by sharing God-given resources."[17] Mass-produced discipleship and leadership development methodologies might prove insufficient to get the job done. Instead, mentors who know how to discern how someone is wired and how they can best contribute to the mission could be vital for accomplishing this task.

Finally, as women and men find themselves in mixed-gender ministry partnerships, they should pursue frank conversations about who can or should be responsible for what. Dividing responsibilities in alignment with each partner's gifting and temperament—and not automatically by gender—should result in partnerships that are both personally satisfying and missionally effective. As communities embrace the perspective that differences are useful for the sake of our mission, as they focus on developing individuals into who they are uniquely wired to be, and as they establish tailored job roles and descriptions, they should see mixed-gender ministry partnerships flourish more fully in their midst.

FINAL THOUGHTS

In one particular research interview, I sat with a long-serving leader. This man had seen and done it all, and his ministry career had been marked by a fervent commitment to flourishing mixed-gender ministry partnerships. In fact, he was so serious about partnership that he and a mixed-gender group of like-minded leaders would meet twice a year specifically for the purpose of learning how to partner more effectively as women and men. That practice

---

[17]Paul D. Stanley and J. Robert Clinton, *Connecting: The Mentoring Relationships You Need to Succeed in Life* (Colorado Springs: NavPress, 1992), 12. Stanley and Clinton identify seven mentoring types: discipler, spiritual guide, coach, counselor, teacher, model, and sponsor.

was unique in all the interviews that I conducted for this research project. When I asked what motivated him to invest so much time and energy in this topic during his time in ministry, he spoke directly to this attribute: "There was this sense that one plus one equals three, not one plus one equals two or one and a half."

The literature, my research, and the Scriptures concur with this assessment. When individuals and communities discern ways to recognize and leverage difference, they may well find their mission expanding exponentially. There is great power in difference.

PROCESSING QUESTIONS

1. How have you seen God use differences to expand the mission in your context?

2. How do you personally fit the stereotypical depiction of your gender? How do you not fit? How do you feel about this?

3. What would need to change for your community to recognize and value difference?

4. What practical things can you or your community do to leverage difference to move your mission forward?

7

VALUE FOR HOLISTIC FRIENDSHIPS

IN COMMUNITY CULTURES THAT ENDORSE FLOURISHING mixed-gender ministry partnerships, my research makes the case that women and men share more than a physical workspace. Indeed, many of those surveyed noted that thriving partnerships are simultaneously holistic friendships. Christian history offers us at least one example of a mixed-gender ministry partnership marked by a legitimate friendship—that of Boniface and Lioba.

Born in 675, Wynfrith of Crediton, later known as Boniface, was an Anglo-Saxon monk who has been called the apostle of Germany. Boniface is known for his many ministry achievements, including church reform, spreading the Benedictine rule, and founding a number of monasteries, most notably the large one in the city of Fulda.

To be sure, Boniface had a long and fruitful ministry career. When he was eighty years old, Boniface left his administrative responsibilities to return to the mission field, where he was eventually martyred, along with fifty companions. On top of all his accomplishments, history also tells us that Boniface was an advocate for a woman named Lioba.

Called out of an English monastery, Lioba eventually became the abbess of the monastic community in Bischofsheim. During her years in ministry, Lioba became known for her rich knowledge of the Bible, canon law, and the works of the early church. Beyond that, Lioba's ministry was marked by the establishment of a number of daughter houses around Germany. One biographer describes the fruit of Lioba's leadership as "good seed over new-plowed fields."[1]

In an era when women were systematically relegated to the cultural margins, it is noteworthy that Boniface respected and empowered a woman like Lioba,

---

[1] Eleanor McLaughlin, "Women, Power, and the Pursuit of Holiness in Medieval Christianity," in *Women of Spirit: Female Leadership in the Jewish and Christian Traditions*, ed. Rosemary Ruether and Eleanor McLaughlin (Eugene, OR: Wipf & Stock, 1998), 105.

affirming her gifts and celebrating her leadership and influence. More than that, Boniface saw himself as a true friend and partner to Lioba.[2]

Indeed, as his life neared its end, Boniface made a strange request of his monks—namely, that he and Lioba would share a tomb together after their deaths. According to the authors of *Constants in Context*, Boniface's unusual request came because "as they had shared in the same missionary partnership, they might wait together for the resurrection."[3] Surely, one would only want to spend eternity alongside someone valued not only because of their ministry partnership but because of their friendship as well.

Boniface and Lioba offer a beautiful and countercultural testimony to the power of ministry partnerships between women and men in general and to the importance of friendship in the process of forming flourishing mixed-gender ministry partnerships in particular.

WOMEN AND MEN AS FRIENDS IN THE RESEARCH

Like these two saints from history, my research suggests that when community cultures affirm the value of holistic friendships between women and men, flourishing mixed-gender ministry partnerships are more likely to become a reality.

At one level, this can mean being present in one another's lives apart from the demands of ministry. During my research process, I interviewed one pair of ministry partners who mentioned that they met weekly, even if there was nothing on the ministry agenda. In fact, they told me that they enjoyed their times together more when they were agenda free, because it provided more room to catch up and connect with one another. This weekly relational connection was vital for their ministry partnership as well as for their friendship.

Further, interviewees indicated that having a holistic friendship can mean being engaged with their partner's family context. In one participant-observation study, I joined a team meeting where a young mother was

---

[2]It is possible that readers are registering a bit of skepticism, thinking that perhaps the relationship between Boniface and Lioba had a romantic dimension that has been ignored or overlooked. This is certainly a possibility, though the historical record gives no hint of such a thing. Instead, skepticism about this friendship being exclusively platonic might say more about the lenses we have developed for mixed-gender friendships than anything else. As will be noted later in this chapter, by and large the church has imbibed the narrative that women and men simply cannot build platonic friendships.

[3]Stephen B. Bevans and Roger Schroeder, *Constants in Context: A Theology of Mission for Today* (New York: Orbis, 2004),125.

present with her newborn. To my surprise, over the course of the meeting, nearly every person took turns holding the baby. This not only gave the mother a break, but it also communicated the team's acceptance and appreciation for the presence of that young mother and her baby in the meeting. Similarly, other interviewees recounted stories of sharing holidays together, going on double dates with spouses, and having their teammates serve as honorary aunts and uncles for their kids. As one longtime leader noted, "If someone feels like you're deeply involved in their story and what the Lord is doing in their lives, it's very fulfilling."

Over the years, I have been a part of many communities that have embraced a culture marked by holistic friendships. I have been prayer partners with my friend Suzy, I have swapped babysitting duties with my friend Layla, and I have trained for marathons with my friend Tina. I cannot think of a single aspect of my life that hasn't been touched in some way by a female coworker who has also become a friend. Recently, I went through a difficult job-change process. Recognizing the complexity of the situation for my whole family, my coworkers rallied around us. Most significantly, one female coworker reached out to my wife to check and see how she was doing in the midst of the process, thus communicating the strong friendship we had built over time. When community cultures are marked by a value for holistic friendships between women and men, mixed-gender ministry partnerships are more likely to flourish.

Women and Men as Friends in Scripture

An examination of Paul's letters reveals his penchant for forming significant friendships with those with whom he served. We find traces of these friendships in the affectionate language that Paul uses to describe his partners. Time and again, Paul gushes about those he has mentored, served with, and worked alongside. Indeed, what is noteworthy is not that Paul expresses this level of affection but that he does so with both the men *and* the women in his life.

For instance, the final chapter of Paul's letter to the church in Rome contains references to twenty-eight of Paul's spiritual siblings, ten of whom were women. From the affectionate language that Paul uses in greeting these women, we can discern the presence of real friendship. For example, consider Phoebe. As will be covered extensively in chapter eight, many scholars believe Phoebe partnered with Paul as the bearer of the actual letter to the church in

Rome, and Paul refers to her as "our sister" (Romans 16:1). Beyond these attributes, Paul also dubs Phoebe a "benefactor of many and of myself as well" (Romans 16:2). The Greek word for "benefactor" in this case is *prostatis*, which can be translated helper, guardian, succorer, or "friend" (NEB).[4]

Or there is Persis, a woman who, according to Paul, "has worked hard in the Lord" (Romans 16:12). Not only that but Persis is described as Paul's "dear friend" (NIV). Indeed, the Greek word used in this verse is *agapētēn*, which can also be translated "beloved." "'The beloved Persis' reveals a close relationship [with Paul] that also implies a corresponding relationship to the Roman believers. . . . She is beloved by the Roman believers as well as Paul."[5] Is there a mixed-gender ministry partnership between Paul and Persis? There certainly is. And one reason it flourishes is because they are dear friends.

Finally, there is Rufus's mother. While we don't know this woman's name, we do know that Paul considered her family, as he dubs her someone who has been "a mother to me also" (Romans 16:13). As it turns out, Paul was a man who lived and ministered within a broad cohort of spiritual sisters (and mothers!). From Romans 16 and elsewhere, we get the impression that Paul would have plenty of spiritual sisters with whom he would aspire to wait for the resurrection.

BENEFITS OF FORMING HOLISTIC MIXED-GENDER FRIENDSHIPS

As communities develop a cultural value for holistic mixed-gender friendships, we can expect at least three benefits to emerge in their ministry contexts. First, as noted in chapter two, we are fundamentally relational beings, and this attribute directly addresses this core aspect of our identity. We are created to feel seen, known, and valued, and friendships tend to provide for these needs in our lives. As a 2018 National Institutes of Health report states, "There is substantial evidence in the psychological and sociological literature that individuals with richer networks of active social relationships tend to be more satisfied and happier with their lives."[6] Without question, people flourish when they have good friends.

---

[4]Jeff Miller, "What Can We Say About Phoebe?," *Priscilla Papers*, April 30, 2011, www.cbeinternational .org/resources/article/priscilla-papers/what-can-we-say-about-phoebe.

[5]Susan Mathew, *Women in the Greetings of Romans 16.1-16: A Study of Mutuality and Women's Ministry in the Letter to the Romans* (New York: Bloomsbury Academic, 2013), 110.

[6]Viviana Amati et al., "Social Relations and Life Satisfaction: The Role of Friends," *Genus* 74, no. 1 (2018): 7. doi:10.1186/s41118-018-0032-z.

Beyond meeting this foundational relational need, a second benefit can be an increase in morale. As noted in chapter one, half the concept of flourishing is personal satisfaction, and this particular attribute contributes to that in a significant way. Frequently, participants in my research expressed joy at the recollection of a ministry partner who over time had become a real friend.

In his book *Reclaiming Friendship*, Ajith Fernando makes the case that our work colleagues are actually some of the best people for us to become friends with. He writes, "Those we are close to are those who can best help us grow. They know us best and can help us in an ongoing way as we go through our day-to-day lives. It is sometimes uncomfortable to live with such helpers, but it is much more effective as an agent for good in our lives."[7] Having workplaces become "agents for good in our lives" through the presence of friends should go a long way toward growing organizational morale.[8]

Finally, holistic friendships offer opportunities for women and men to develop trust in their ministry partnerships. Really knowing someone opens the door for greater relational trust, which can come in handy when there is internal conflict or when a partnership is under external pressure. To be able to access a reservoir of trust will enable women and men to work together more efficiently and effectively.

Not long ago, I directed a conference in partnership with my ministry partner Melissa. The trust embedded in our friendship, forged over the course of some fifteen years of working together, came in handy when the conference facility couldn't deliver what we needed. We had a short conversation and then went our separate ways to solve the problem, trusting one another to get our jobs done. In the end, we solved the problem and the conference ultimately succeeded. These three benefits—meeting relational needs, greater morale, and deeper trust—are available as communities embrace this value for holistic mixed-gender friendships.

---

[7]Ajith Fernando, *Reclaiming Friendship: Relating to Each Other in a Frenzied World* (Harrisonburg, VA: Herald, 1993), 48.

[8]To be sure, Fernando's perspective finds plenty of opposition. The Drucker quote mentioned later in this chapter is one example, and in one forum on the Manager Tools website there is a robust exposition of the perils of hiring friends as coworkers: https://www.manager-tools.com/forums /thoughts-hiring-friends. Still, Fernando's perspective also resonates with research conducted by Gallup in their 2017 *State of the American Workplace* report: "Early research on employee engagement and the elements revealed a unique social pattern among employees in top performing teams. When employees possess a deep sense of affiliation with their team members, they are driven to take positive actions that benefit the business—actions they may not otherwise even consider." See www.gallup.com/workplace/238085/state-american-workplace-report-2017.aspx.

Barriers to Building Holistic Mixed-Gender Friendships

Since this attribute resides in the community culture domain, it is worth examining how the cultures of our churches, communities, and organizations might work against the formation of holistic friendships between women and men in a ministry context. I can identify five potential roadblocks.

First, we must talk about fear. Far too many leaders and organizations have had to endure the trauma of a leader's lapse in judgment and the resulting relational carnage. This has resulted in a relational climate marked by fear, specifically the fear of what might happen sexually if a mixed-gender ministry partnership or friendship crosses the line.

This is a fear that exists in the larger culture as well. In the 1989 movie *When Harry Met Sally*, Billy Crystal's character famously tells Meg Ryan's character that mixed-gender friendships are impossible, because, inevitably, "the sex part always gets in the way."[9] Critiquing this idea in *The Book of Womanhood*, Amy Davis Abdullah writes, "Harry was wrong. And though his assertion has pervaded society, we can seek opportunities to enter conversations and partnerships with other men and women as the fiery work of the Holy Spirit restores our 'creational DNA,' the image of the triune God."[10]

Without question, there is much at stake in this area. Our gospel witness mandates purity and health in our mixed-gender friendships. But we must not give in to the fear of what might happen as women and men form mixed-gender friendships in their pursuit of flourishing ministry partnerships. Instead, individuals and communities should pursue intentional conversations about contextualized boundaries (see chap. 10).

A second barrier to the formation of holistic friendships in our communities can be a rigid application of work/life balance. Much has been written recently about the importance of having a firm wall between a person's work and the rest of their life. For instance, Bryan Dyson, former COO of Coca-Cola, writes,

> Imagine life as a game in which you are juggling some five balls in the air. You name them—work, family, health, friends and spirit and you're keeping all of these in the air. You will soon understand that work is a rubber ball. If you drop it, it will bounce back. But the other four balls—family, health, friends, and spirit—are made of glass. If you drop one of these, they will be irrevocably

---

[9]*When Harry Met Sally*, directed by Rob Reiner (Beverly Hills, CA: Castle Rock Entertainment, 1989).
[10]Amy F. Davis Abdullah, *The Book of Womanhood* (Eugene, OR: Cascade, 2015), 146.

scuffed, marked, nicked, damaged, or even shattered. They will never be the same. You must understand that and strive for balance in your life.[11]

While we should indeed endeavor to avoid becoming workaholics, we need to also resist the temptation to construct an impenetrable barrier between our work and the rest of our lives. It is possible to have room in our lives for vital friendships both inside and outside of our work.

Third, this value for holistic friendships can clash with necessary organizational realties. When ministry partners become friends, personnel processes can make things tricky, and that is especially true when there is a power dynamic in the working partnership. In *The Daily Drucker*, management guru Peter Drucker writes, "A CEO who has 'friendships' within the company, has 'social relations' with colleagues, or discusses anything with them except the job, cannot remain impartial—or at least, which is equally damaging, he will not appear as such. Loneliness, distance and formality may be contrary to his temperament—but they are his duty."[12]

I have experienced this barrier in my own ministry life. I supervised my friend Layla for about a decade, even as we developed a robust friendship during our time working together. Still, every spring I had to write Layla's performance review. Early on, my temptation was to pull punches because of our friendship. Thankfully, we recognized this dynamic, and talking about it helped to diffuse it. By the end of our time working in a supervisorial partnership, Layla and I had flipped the dynamic; as friends, we learned that we *wanted* to give each other constructive feedback, and the trust we developed allowed us to do so effectively.

Fourth, there is a question about capacity. It is unrealistic to think that we can become best friends with each of our coworkers. While this attribute calls for some degree of friendship with each coworker, it is also true that relationships will look different from partnership to partnership. Given that reality, partners should be careful to not show favoritism to those with whom they have closer friendships, and that is particularly true when a supervisorial dynamic is present.

---

[11]Heike Young, "9 Thought-Provoking Quotes About Work-Life Balance," *Salesforce*, July 8, 2015, https://medium.com/@salesforce/9-thought-provoking-quotes-about-work-life-balance-64673dea0747.

[12]See the entry for April 14 in Peter F. Drucker, *The Daily Drucker: 366 Days of Insight and Motivation for Getting the Right Things Done* (New York: Harper Business, 2004). I opted to leave the generic masculine pronouns in Drucker's quote as one more illustration of the default assumption that the CEO of a major corporation would, of course, be a man.

A final challenge to growing a value for holistic friendships in a community's culture is a lack of models. Generally, aspiring mixed-gender ministry partners will suffer from a lack of examples. For too long, fear-gripped faith communities have opted to avoid permitting mixed-gender friendships, instead opting to focus on the marriage context. This means that as the culture shifts to promote such friendships, communities will need to major on learning what works and what doesn't in this area.[13]

BUILDING A VALUE FOR HOLISTIC MIXED-GENDER FRIENDSHIPS

How might communities go about shifting their cultures to overcome these barriers and actively promote the value of holistic friendships between women and men? First, communities must make space to talk about mixed-gender friendships. As has been noted previously, the church's silence on gender issues in general and mixed-gender friendships in particular has been deafening. Aimee Byrd writes, "I'd love to be able to point the secular culture to Christ's church as a representation of how communion with God affects relationships between the sexes. But we've reduced a lot of the discussion about manhood in the church to how a man shows authority. Much of the discussion about womanhood draws lines nitpicking what a woman can do and she can't do. And the church has provided little discussion about how men and women relate to each other."[14] People in our faith communities will benefit from safe spaces to talk about how mixed-gender friendships are working or could be working in context. Setting aside an evening to work through the questions at the end of this chapter would be an easy place for any community to start.

Next, our communities need a fresh vision for mixed-gender friendships. I propose the notion of siblingship as a governing paradigm for thinking about friendships between women and men. It worked for Paul and his community, and it ought to work for us as well. Noting that the sibling language appears

---

[13]Interestingly, there is evidence to suggest that the coming generation, called iGen or Generation Z in the literature, is arriving with a predisposition toward mixed-gender ministry partnerships as well as mixed-gender friendships. As a group, they are instinctively inclusive. In her book on iGen, Jean M. Twenge writes, "From LGBT identities to gender to race, iGen'ers expect equality and are often surprised, even shocked, to still encounter prejudice." As Generation Z gains cultural voice, it would be wonderful if they could be mentored by prior generations who have figured out how to be friends and partners in healthy ways. Jean M. Twenge, *iGen: Why Today's Super-Connected Kids Are Growing Up Less Rebellious, More Tolerant, Less Happy—and Completely Unprepared for Adulthood* (New York: Atria, 2017), 227.

[14]Aimee Byrd, *Why Can't We Be Friends?: Avoidance Is Not Purity* (Phillipsburg, NJ: P&R, 2018), 25.

118 times in Paul's writings, New Testament scholar Joseph Hellerman writes, "The idea of the church as family is ubiquitous in Paul's writing and is, therefore, central to Paul's understanding of the manner in which interpersonal relationships are to function in the communities to which he writes."[15] Embracing the biblical model of "brothers and sisters" should help our communities establish healthy friendships in greater measure.

Many writers have encouraged the church to adopt this concept of spiritual siblingship. For instance, the authors of *Mixed Ministry* note that "healthy ministry requires community—a family serving God together. And friendships between men and women are a part of the picture. Loving one another as siblings is not optional if we want to do God's work, God's way—as a spiritual family of friends."[16] Choosing to think of one another as spiritual siblings can go a long way toward mitigating the fears described earlier. Siblingship offers "a respectful way to relate to one another—and, when we relate this way, we remove the possibility of sex."[17] Helping those in our communities envision someone from the opposite gender as, first and foremost, a brother or sister in Christ can pave the way toward flourishing mixed-gender friendships and ministry partnerships.

Finally, we must practically equip people to be good friends. In too many circles, friendship seems to be a lost art. A 2006 study cosponsored by Duke University and the University of Arizona notes that "Americans' circle of confidants has shrunk dramatically in the past two decades and the number of people who say they have no one with whom to discuss important matters has more than doubled."[18]

In light of this reality, people need training in basic communication skills such as asking good questions and listening well (see chap. 9). In addition, they should seek to become proficient in adopting a learner's posture (see chap. 2). And as noted in the research above, individuals can pursue, with permission, relationships with their colleague's spouse and family members. As people become more familiar and comfortable with these tools, we can expect a shift in culture toward a fundamental value for holistic friendships, and flourishing mixed-gender ministry partnerships should follow.

---

[15]Joseph Hellerman, *The Ancient Church as Family* (Sheffield: Sheffield Phoenix, 2007), 92.

[16]Sue Edwards, Kelley Matthews, and Henry J. Rogers, *Mixed Ministry: Working Together as Sisters and Brothers in an Oversexed Society* (Grand Rapids, MI: Kregel Academic and Professional, 2008), 84.

[17]Byrd, *Why Can't We Be Friends?*, 14.

[18]"Americans Have Fewer Friends Outside the Family, Duke Study Shows," *Duke Today*, June 23, 2006, https://today.duke.edu/2006/06/socialisolation.html.

FINAL THOUGHTS

At times, when I asked participants about the mixed-gender partnerships that they had enjoyed during their time in ministry, they would tear up. On occasion, this was because the question surfaced feelings of pain and regret. More often, it was because the story they were about to tell me was about someone whose ministry partnership had also become a friendship.

Reflecting on her long-running partnership with a man in her organization, one woman wiped away tears and said, "I care about what's happening in his full life, and he cares about what's happening in my full life." That is a beautiful picture of a holistic friendship, one that no doubt Boniface and Lioba would approve of.

PROCESSING QUESTIONS

1. What is your gut reaction to the notion of mixed-gender ministry partnerships also becoming holistic friendships?

2. Which benefits compel you to consider building this attribute into both your personal experience as well as your community's culture?

3. Which barriers do you identify with?

4. Give the culture of your church, community, or organization a letter grade for this attribute. Why that grade?

5. What is one thing you can do this week to build a more authentic friendship with a person from the opposite gender that you are in partnership with?

8

CORPORATE SENSITIVITY TO ADVERSE
GENDER DYNAMICS

Several years ago, my colleague Layla and I met with a prominent local pastor to invite his support of our ministry with InterVarsity. Layla had taken risks and done all of the hard work to set up the meeting, including making the initial contact and clarifying the meeting's purpose. Then, she invited me to come, with the thought that I could cast a larger vision for our ministry, thus encouraging this pastor to support our work more significantly.

Once we arrived at our local diner and made introductions, Layla began her pitch, and that is when the meeting got awkward. From the moment Layla started talking, this pastor only had eyes for me. His eyes never left me, no matter what I tried. I began intentionally breaking eye contact, looking at the table, my notes, or in my backpack. I even purposefully dropped my pen in an effort to break eye contact. Nothing worked. Next, I tried verbal cues, noting that Layla could speak to whatever it was we were talking about, and then turning in my chair to face her. No change. Finally, I got up and went to the bathroom, only to return to his eye contact, patiently waiting for me.

Once the meeting was done and the pastor had left, Layla and I stayed after to debrief. Of course, we had both noticed the pastor's inability—or unwillingness—to make eye contact with Layla, but from there we had two different reactions. For me, it was simply off-putting. It was odd to have spent an hour being stared at, especially when it was Layla's meeting. For Layla, it was far worse. The experience of being ignored during the appointment—her appointment—had wounded her deeply, and the tears that flowed demonstrated that being minimized in that way had inflicted significant pain. Our meeting that day ended with me seeking to care for and support my sister.

My research suggests that mixed-gender ministry partnerships are more likely to flourish when the community cultures in which they are situated exhibit an awareness of adverse gender dynamics—dynamics that particularly marginalize women. When communities develop a radar for such dynamics, they are able to proactively mitigate them, and mixed-gender ministry partnerships are more likely to flourish.

CORPORATE SENSITIVITY TO ADVERSE GENDER DYNAMICS IN THE SCRIPTURES

This idea of a corporate sensitivity to adverse gender dynamics is demonstrated in the New Testament partnership of Paul and Phoebe. As noted previously, many scholars think that Phoebe was the bearer of the apostle Paul's letter to the church in Rome. For instance, John Stott writes, "It seems very likely that Phoebe was entrusted with the responsible task of carrying Paul's letter to its destination in Rome."[1]

Further, there is solid evidence to indicate that Phoebe could well have been the one to read and exposit the letter to the church. Craig Keener writes, "Since she bears Paul's letter, she may be called upon to explain anything ambiguous in the letter when the Romans read it, and Paul wished them to understand that she is indeed qualified to explain his writing."[2] Similarly, in her book on Phoebe, Paula Gooder notes that as Paul's chosen and commissioned courier, she would have been his representative in Rome. And since "the primary way that most Christians would have engaged with any text . . . would have been aurally,"[3] a reasonable conclusion is that the first person to explain the book of Romans apart from Paul would have been Phoebe.

Even though Phoebe was likely Paul's choice to bear and present the letter to the Roman church, she could still have faced significant pushback. In the first century, the Greek social fabric consisted of two spheres, the more valued public sphere, which was largely the domain of men and their civic engagement, and the private sphere, which was essentially the domain of housebound women who were expected to care for the family. In *Politics*, Aristotle provides the rationale for this hierarchical stratification of public and private spheres, noting, "As regards male and female, the former is superior, the latter

---

[1]John Stott, *Romans: God's Good News for the World* (Downers Grove, IL: InterVarsity Press, 1994), 392. In a poetic take on Phoebe's role as letter carrier, a French theologian named Rénan is thought to have written that "Phoebe carried under the folds of her robe the whole future of Christian theology."

[2]Craig S. Keener, *Paul, Women, & Wives: Marriage and Women's Ministry in the Letters of Paul* (Peabody, MA: Hendrickson, 1992), 238.

[3]Paula Gooder, *Phoebe: A Story* (Downers Grove, IL: IVP Academic, 2018), 247.

inferior; the male is ruler, the female is subject."[4] So, for Phoebe to step outside of that social framework to present the letter in a public-sphere type of setting could well have raised eyebrows among members of the Roman church.

In light of the pushback Phoebe might have faced as she arrived in Rome with his letter, Paul vouches for his messenger in the letter itself.[5] In Romans 16:1-2, Paul writes: "I commend to you our sister Phoebe, a deacon of the church at Cenchreae, so that you may welcome her in the Lord as is fitting for the saints, and help her in whatever she may require from you, for she has been a benefactor of many and of myself as well." With this twofold recitation of Phoebe's resume, Paul effectively blocks potential objections to her leadership.

First, Paul identifies Phoebe as a deacon from the church in Cenchreae. The Greek word for "deacon" carries the implications of someone who serves or ministers to others. In short, Paul is identifying Phoebe as a titled church leader. In his essay "What Can We Say About Phoebe?," Jeff Miller argues that Paul's usage of *diakonos* in the text carries with it the notion of leadership office. He writes, "Phoebe's description as *diakonos* includes the qualifying phrase 'of the congregation in Cenchreae.' This localization of Phoebe's position strongly suggests Paul had in mind a specific status rather than general comportment."[6]

In addition to citing Phoebe's leadership role in the church in Cenchreae, Paul also testifies to her generosity and care for others by calling her a "benefactor of many." Reflecting on the implications of this aspect of Phoebe's identity, theologian Marg Mowczko writes, "As well as being an important part of Roman society at all levels, patronage was also important in the church.

---

[4]Aristotle, *Politics*, in *The Philosophy of Aristotle*, trans. J. L. Creed and A. E. Wardman (New York, NY: Penguin Group, 2011), 436. Katelyn Beaty tracks this notion of separate spheres, noting that "the idea that 'a woman's place is in the home' can be found in ancient Greek culture, traditional Judaism, and Christianity. But it became enshrined as moral and spiritual fact among relatively wealthy Americans in the nineteenth century." Lamenting the impact of this ideology on women, Beaty writes, "Calling work masculine and relationships and networking feminine . . . threatens to keep women from knowing the good and holy purposes of work, whether inside the home or outside of it." *A Woman's Place: A Christian Vision for Your Calling in the Office, the Home, and the World* (New York: Howard, 2016), 105-6, 110.

[5]Letters of recommendation were fairly typical in antiquity. "Jewish travelers normally carried letters of recommendation attesting that they should be received; they were generally bearers of such letters themselves. (The only mail service was by imperial couriers for the government; Paul thus had to send the letter by a traveler.)" Craig S. Keener, *The IVP Bible Background Commentary* (Downers Grove, IL: InterVarsity Press, 1993), 447.

[6]Jeff Miller, "What Can We Say About Phoebe?," *Priscilla Papers*, April 30, 2011, https://www.cbeinternational.org/resources/article/priscilla-papers/what-can-we-say-about-phoebe.

Edwin Judge has remarked, 'Christianity was a movement sponsored by local patrons to their social dependents.'"[7]

In our day, many communities emphasize a visiting presenter's credentials before they speak. Job titles, academic honorifics, significant experiences, and notable publications tend to be included in such an introduction. This establishes the speaker as an authority on the topic with those in attendance. Similarly, by citing these two aspects of Phoebe's identity—her leadership role and her catalyzing of the church's mission through her generous patronage—Paul cuts off potential objections to her leadership in the church in Rome, thus inviting those who will receive her to be more open to her influence. In this way, Paul identifies a potential adverse gender dynamic and seeks to mitigate it before it can bear toxic fruit in Phoebe's ministry in Rome.

CORPORATE SENSITIVITY TO ADVERSE GENDER DYNAMICS IN THE RESEARCH

Like Paul with Phoebe, when individuals and communities are able to look ahead and anticipate adverse gender dynamics, they become able to more effectively mitigate them. When that happens, women experience less organizational trauma, and mixed-gender ministry partnerships can flourish in greater measure. In my study, this process of identifying and mitigating adverse gender dynamics played out differently for women and men.

Many of the men I interviewed told stories of coming to grips with the reality that gender dynamics often work in their favor. Generally speaking, the social and organizational playing fields tilt in favor of men, and a growing consciousness of that reality matters a great deal. One male supervisor noted that "not realizing that you have a bias or even a prejudice . . . can be detrimental." And reflecting on missteps in his mixed-gender ministry partnerships, another male leader ruefully recalled "boneheaded statements that came back to haunt me."

These things noted, when men were able to develop an awareness of adverse gender dynamics, they were then able to mitigate them ahead of time. In one case, a male supervisor described a conversation he was having with a female colleague as they walked through a mall. As it happened, this man was significantly taller than the woman he was talking to, and when he got on

---

[7]Marg Mowczko, "Wealthy Women in the First-Century Roman World and in the Church," blog, April 19, 2017, https://margmowczko.com/wealthy-women-roman-world-and-church/.

first at an escalator, that height difference was only accentuated. Realizing that a superior height difference is one physical feature that can adversely affect gender dynamics,[8] this leader paused the conversation and recommended they switch places on the escalator. While I am sure it was awkward to shuffle past one another in order to change places on the escalator, this gesture acknowledged the subtle but potentially adverse dynamics at play in the situation.

In another case, a veteran female leader related a story of her former supervisor, who saw a problem on the horizon and took proactive steps to prevent it. After a particularly successful conference, their organization decided to reward employees by buying and sending neckties as thank-you gifts. When this woman's male supervisor heard this, he quickly realized that he would have a problem, as this woman was the sole woman on his leadership team. As a result, he spent days before their upcoming team meeting driving around to various department stores in his town on a quest to find a scarf that approximated the color and pattern of the neckties. In the end, he was successful, and he presented it to her at the same time he passed out the ties. More than forty years on from this moment, this woman recounted this story through tears, concluding with, "I still have that scarf, honestly."

In contrast to the experiences of many men, almost all the women surveyed were hyperaware of the negative gender dynamics operating under the surface, both in interpersonal and corporate settings. For instance, one female leader shared that every time she prepares to go to a national meeting, she carefully considers how she will present herself, particularly in terms of her wardrobe.[9] Perhaps it need not be said, but no male interviewee related a similar story. In addition, several women pointed out the relative dearth of women leaders in upper-level management positions, exposing the reality of structural or systemic tripwires.

---

[8]MaryKate Morse's book, *Making Room for Leadership: Power, Space and Influence* (Downers Grove, IL: InterVarsity Press, 2008), was also referenced in chap. 5 in the context of the attribute of freely shared power. This story demonstrates the reality that size and stature can be a factor in how much space a person takes up.

[9]Joanne Lipman asserts that wardrobe is just one of many unique considerations for women in the workplace. "It takes hours of effort and hundreds of tiny daily conscious and subconscious decisions about what to say, when to speak, what to wear, whether to acknowledge we have a sick kid at home—moves we make to protect ourselves and that are completely invisible to most men." *That's What She Said: What Men Need to Know (and Women Need to Tell Them) About Working Together* (New York: William Morrow, 2018), 6.

For both men and women, solving the problem of adverse gender dynamics begins with diagnosing them in the first place, and doing that depends on a community culture that is attuned to what is happening under the surface. As those adverse gender dynamics are spotted, the community can do something to prevent or fix them.

A TAXONOMY OF ADVERSE GENDER DYNAMICS

The above stories detail several examples of adverse gender dynamics, but there are unfortunately many more. In their groundbreaking research, Amy Diehl and Leanne Dzubinski articulated twenty-seven examples of what they label "unconscious gender bias." Culling data collected from women executives in the higher education and faith-based nonprofit occupational sectors, the authors conclude that "these barriers are deeply embedded in organizational structures and functions, rendering them at times virtually invisible."[10] For Diehl and Dzubinski, such barriers exist at three levels: individual, organizational, and societal.

First, the authors identify what they label "individual barriers," internal blocks that can hold back women in the workplace. These include:

- Communication style restraints, where women feel the burden of communicating in ways that will make them be seen more favorably by others

- Conscious unconsciousness, where women make choices to simply ignore or disregard adverse gender dynamics in the workplace

- Personalizing, where women assume personal responsibility for organizational or systemic failures

- Psychological glass ceiling, where women underplay their own abilities

- Work-life conflict, where women face unique challenges in balancing their personal and professional responsibilities

At an organizational level, the authors cite sixteen different examples of adverse gender dynamics. "These barriers represent ways of discounting women's leadership contributions and limiting their organizational effectiveness."[11] These are:

---

[10]Amy Diehl and Leanne Dzubinski, "Making the Invisible Visible: A Cross-Sector Analysis of Gender-Based Leadership Barriers," in *Human Resource Development Quarterly* 27, no. 2 (Summer 2016), 203.
[11]Diehl and Dzubinski, "Making the Invisible Visible," 191.

- Devaluing of communal practice, where communal activities often performed by women, such as note taking in meetings, are discounted in the workplace
- Discrimination, where women are denied access or opportunities by virtue of their gender
- Exclusion from informal networks, where women are not invited to male-only activities outside of work
- Glass cliff, where women are assigned roles with a significant risk of failure
- Lack of mentoring, where women are denied the chance to have an organizational mentor
- Lack of sponsorship, where women are denied a sponsor who can provide the organizational resources necessary for them to be successful
- Lack of support, where women are given a task but not the resources to do the job
- Male gatekeeping, where men control the participation and leadership of women in the workplace
- Male organizational culture, where the workplace culture is stereotypically masculine
- Organizational ambivalence, where words and actions communicate a lack of confidence in a woman's ability to accomplish the task
- Queen bee effect, where successful women block other women from advancement in an effort to maintain their own position
- Salary inequality, where women are paid less than their male colleagues
- Tokenism, where just enough women are promoted for the organization to feel like it can label itself "diverse" in terms of gender
- Two-person career structure, where one spouse is employed by the organization but the other has (unpaid) obligations as well
- Unequal standards, where women are held to higher standards than their male colleagues
- Workplace harassment, where women are made to endure toxic behaviors that threaten or undermine their leadership or personhood

A third set of adverse gender dynamics in the workplace occur at the societal level, the broadest domain reviewed by the study's authors. There are six barriers at the societal level:

- Control of women's voices, where restrictions are placed on the contribution of women in various conversations

- Cultural restraints of women's own choices, where women find themselves limited in terms of their social or vocational options

- Gender stereotypes, with unyielding cultural expectations about women

- Gender unconsciousness, where there is lack of awareness about the role that gender plays in a given context

- Leadership perceptions, where effective leadership is exclusively associated with stereotypical masculinity

- Scrutiny, where there is an undue focus on women and their contributions

These twenty-seven dynamics can be difficult to spot. Often they are subtle, lurking below the surface at each of the three levels. Communities can benefit from a list like this one, as it provides them with specific adverse gender dynamics to watch out for.

BENEFITS OF CORPORATE SENSITIVITY TO ADVERSE GENDER DYNAMICS

There are clear benefits to a community developing a radar for detecting adverse gender dynamics. First, as communities develop this sensitivity, we can expect women to experience greater freedom. In her book *Emboldened*, Pastor Tara Beth Leach offers a compelling vision for empowered and released women in ministry: "Now is the time for women to claim their full callings and be freed from gender-based restrictions. Now is the time for women to rise up and use their God-given gifts with boldness. Now is the time for the church to no longer be lopsided, but to move forward in its full potential, with men and women serving alongside one another—unhindered."[12] If we want to see the Genesis vision of gender equality become a reality for women in our communities, we would do well to interrogate and dismantle the adverse dynamics that so often oppress them.

---

[12]Tara Beth Leach, *Emboldened: A Vision for Empowering Women in Ministry* (Downers Grove, IL: InterVarsity Press, 2017), 189.

Second, as communities and ministry teams overcome the adverse dynamics that lurk below the surface, we should expect them to increase in productivity. In other words, their missional effectiveness should increase as women and men function more collaboratively as partners. Writing to men in her book *We*, business leadership coach and speaker Rania Anderson notes that "a gender-diverse team is a competitive advantage. It may seem counter-intuitive, but when you accelerate the success of women, you accelerate your own success. If you are able to build a high-performing diverse team, your results will outpace your competition."[13] For more on this idea, see chapter six on differences for the sake of mission.

Finally, continuing to work hard at developing a communal sensitivity to adverse gender dynamics should result in increasing awareness over time. Joanne Lipman notes, "Wherever you stand, once you see the gap—women being overlooked, interrupted, their ideas credited to a man—you'll notice it everywhere."[14]

My own journey demonstrates this particular benefit. The more aware I have become of these under-the-surface dynamics, the quicker I have become to notice and then mitigate them. Not long ago, I was copied on an email from our corporate headquarters to my teammate Jenn. Because we had talked about the possibility of that email coming, I knew that she was not interested in responding in the affirmative to the question being asked. So, in a spirit of advocacy, I responded to the email right away and, in my mind, I solved the problem.

The next day, however, I started to wonder if my jumping in had been the right course of action, so I reached out to Jenn. As it turned out, she had been hurt by my choice to respond first. Gently, she explained to me that I had usurped her agency. Simply put, that was her email to write. While I wish I had caught the adverse dynamic in real time, I was glad that I caught it eventually. In the same way, as communities intentionally pursue greater awareness regarding these adverse gender dynamics, the more effective they should become at seeing and then mitigating them.

---

[13]Rania Anderson, *We: Men, Women, and the Decisive Formula for Winning at Work* (Hoboken, NJ: Wiley, 2018), 33.

[14]Lipman, *That's What She Said*, 17.

BARRIERS TO A CORPORATE SENSITIVITY TO ADVERSE
GENDER DYNAMICS

Unfortunately, there are at least three barriers to communities developing a radar for identifying adverse gender dynamics. For one thing, developing an awareness of adverse gender dynamics requires the ability and willingness to perceive what is really and truly going on. Regrettably, humans tend to struggle with "mindbugs," a term authors Mahzarin R. Banaji and Anthony G. Greenwald use in their book *Blindspot* to explain "ingrained habits of thought that lead to errors in how we perceive, remember, reason, and make decisions."[15] Mindbugs prevent us from seeing our world as it really is.

In this area in particular, mindbugs can limit people from seeing the adverse gender dynamics that are at play both with individuals and in community cultures. In the last several years, "mansplaining" has become a commonly talked about problem in organizational life. A practical example of Dzubinski and Diehl's "control of women's voices" dynamic above, mansplaining describes the phenomenon where a man explains something to a woman in a patronizing or condescending way. A glaring form is when a woman brings expertise and insights to a meeting and gains a hearing—only for a man to jump in, "Well, actually . . ." followed by a "correction" that wrongly claims to understand women's experiences better. I regularly catch mansplaining these days, but I shudder to think about how many times a mindbug caused me to miss it over the years.

Second, developing a radar for adverse gender dynamics requires a commitment to honest and rigorous debrief, and if a community is unable or unwilling to process the reality of their corporate culture through constant debriefing and learning, it is going to be difficult to identify and then mitigate these dynamics. A community can only disempower an adverse gender dynamic if they are willing and able to recognize it in the first place. Often, this process begins with the community choosing to trust and listen to the women who are enduring the pain. That is particularly true the more difficult the dynamics are to spot.

Third, particularly when our meeting culture prioritizes efficiency over all else, it can be difficult to make and protect space to address adverse gender dynamics. In the same way that individuals can opt not to pursue greater self-awareness in terms of their gender brokenness (see chap. 4),

---

[15]Mahzarin R. Banaji and Anthony G. Greenwald, *Blindspot: Hidden Biases of Good People* (London: Bantam, 2016), 4.

communities and teams can make similar choices. After all, it takes time and energy to identify and mitigate adverse dynamics, and often time and energy are in short supply.

The good news is that if a community is able to overcome these three barriers, they will be able to identify and then work to mitigate the adverse dynamics that too often relegate women to the margins in our communities and organizations.

Developing a Corporate Sensitivity to Adverse Gender Dynamics

Communities can take two active steps to develop a sensitivity to adverse gender dynamics. First, communities should pursue education in this area. Communal processing of Diehl and Dzubinski's research findings would be one way to accomplish this. As with the self-awareness attribute from chapter four, the more attuned we are to what is operating beneath the surface, the more we will be able to minimize its effects. Knowing what the possibilities are in terms of adverse gender dynamics is one step toward making that happen. Recently, I coached a leadership team through a process of identifying adverse gender dynamics in their context. Together we read through Diehl and Dzubinski's list, and then they brainstormed concrete examples from their ministry context. Going forward, they now have a collective awareness of what to watch out for as they do their work together.

A second step involves rigorous reflection and debrief. Individuals and groups should mine their experiences for these subtle, negative dynamics. In the research process, many people talked about the importance of a one-on-one debrief. Similar to my experience with Layla following the meeting with that would-be donor, they pointed to the practice of pausing to interpret what they had just experienced and to discern how they might avoid those negative dynamics in the future.

Taking it one step further, one group of leaders recounted one of their communal practices designed to surface and exposit tensions that arise from various subtle dynamics, including adverse gender ones. Their policy was that anyone on the team could pause their team meeting at any time to share what they were feeling or experiencing. While this struck me as a pretty inefficient way to run a meeting—and it would doubtless be awkward at times—it also painted a vivid picture of health. Over time, this group testified that they experienced fewer and fewer pauses, as they called out and then problem solved these adverse dynamics.

As groups major on debriefing their experiences together, the following questions could be beneficial:

- How did we do as a team (or as a partnership) today? Every person can give themselves a letter grade, and then the group can discuss any differences or outliers.

- Were there any points in our conversation where people felt awkward? Why? What was happening under the surface? Is there anything for the group to process together as a community? (If the group is fluent with those twenty-seven dynamics, they can utilize that list as a grid.)

- What did we do well in terms of our communication with one another? What victories can we celebrate? What do we want to continue to do as we work together as women and men?

- Is there anything each of us can be doing between now and our next meeting to become a better ministry partner?

FINAL THOUGHTS

Rania Anderson notes that "today, bias against women is primarily unconscious or manifests in the form of microaggressions that are not fully recognized or understood."[16] Overall, the testimony of those interviewed agrees with Anderson's assertion. Developing a corporate sensitivity to adverse gender dynamics will not just happen. These dynamics are subtle and sneaky, and they take willful work to identify.

Memorably, in his research interview, one leader referenced the 2004 Nicolas Cage movie *National Treasure* when describing these dynamics. In that movie, Cage's character goes on an international hunt for lost treasure, and finding one clue involves a viewing a map while wearing a pair of specially configured Revolutionary War–era spectacles. With the naked eye, Cage's character is unable to read the map he holds in his hand, but when he puts the special glasses on, he is able to see what truth the map really holds. In the same way, when communities choose to pay attention to the subtle adverse gender

---

[16]Anderson, *We*, 69.

dynamics that are lurking under the surface, they can chart a way forward toward flourishing mixed-gender ministry partnerships.

PROCESSING QUESTIONS

1. Which adverse gender dynamics from Diehl and Dzubinski's list have you either personally experienced or seen in practice in your work environment?

2. What adjective(s) would you use to describe the level of your personal sensitivity to detecting adverse gender dynamics? How about for your community? Why those adjectives?

3. What can you do to fortify your community's sensitivity to adverse gender dynamics?

4. What could it look like to mitigate the adverse gender dynamics at play in your community? What might it look like for your community to commit itself to regular and robust debrief in this area?

PART 3

INTENTIONAL
PRACTICES

INTENTIONAL PRACTICES
▲ Abundant Communication
▲ Contextualized Boundaries
▲ Public Affirmation and
Modeling

MIXED-GENDER MINISTRY PARTNERS can have a vibrant inner life, and they can be a part of a community culture that advocates for their ministry partnership, but if they do not take concrete steps toward flourishing mixed-gender ministry partnerships, they are unlikely to reap the rewards that come with partnerships that are both personally satisfying and missionally effective. Truly, to not take action is to miss the chance to experience the joys of God's Genesis design for partnership between the genders.

In his book *Outliers*, Malcolm Gladwell argues that what distinguishes high achievers from others is practice. He writes, "The idea that excellence at performing a complex task requires a critical minimum level of practice surfaces again and again in studies of expertise. In fact, researchers have settled on what they believe is the magic number for true expertise: ten thousand hours."[1]

---

[1]Malcolm Gladwell, *Outliers: The Story of Success* (New York: Little, Brown, 2008), 39. I do not mean to suggest that it will take ten thousand hours for individuals and communities to experience flourishing

To be sure, mixed-gender ministry partnerships will fall into the category of "complex tasks," and so we should not be surprised that they will require plenty of practice. If individuals and communities are going to spend time and effort becoming experts in the area of mixed-gender ministry partnerships, what might they actually do?

While every chapter of this book has suggested concrete action steps, this final section articulates three attributes that emerged in the research as critical intentional practices. When women and men make purposeful choices to practice abundant communication, contextualized boundaries, and public affirmation and modeling, not only will they be on their way to mixed-gender ministry expertise, but they will be more likely to experience flourishing in the mixed-gender ministry partnerships they are a part of.

---

in the context of their mixed-gender ministry partnerships. On the contrary, in my experience, personal satisfaction and missional effectiveness can begin to accrue early on in the partnership.

9

ABUNDANT COMMUNICATION

ONE OF MY STANDARD RESEARCH INTERVIEW questions invited respondents to tell me a story about a time when they felt like a mixed-gender ministry partnership they were involved in had really gone well. In one instance, a female supervisor told me about the very first time she met with a recently hired male supervisee.

Not long after sitting down, she raised the topic of mixed-gender ministry partnerships, asking questions about his past experiences working with women, any concerns he had about reporting to a woman in the ministry context, and whether he had done any thinking about the dynamics of women and men in partnership. By her own admission, the conversation was awkward, and she could observe that it was a bit overwhelming for her new protégé.

On the other hand, for this leader that introductory conversation was vital, and choosing to have it early on signaled that this would be a conversation that would continue as their partnership evolved. In fact, looking back over the interview transcript, she used the word *intentional* five times in her story. It was clear to me that this initial interaction was critically important for this leader.

When I expressed my wonder at her resolve and courage in having this conversation with her new supervisee, she was hasty to connect it to the practice embedded in the culture of the leadership community they were a part of. "I think it's a very natural dynamic on our staff team. [The dynamics of working together as women and men are] something that we talk about on our team. We haven't really had a choice because there's a whole department in our ministry that has nothing but women directors between them and the vice president, so it's something we cannot avoid."

Whether they are forced to by the circumstances of their work, or whether they choose it because it is a wise practice, when individuals and communities communicate clearly, consistently, and vulnerably, their mixed-gender ministry partnerships are more likely to flourish. Abundant communication is a critical intentional practice for building mixed-gender ministry partnerships that are personally satisfying and missionally effective.

ABUNDANT COMMUNICATION IN THE RESEARCH

Alongside the theological conviction attribute, this attribute comes the closest to being a dealbreaker in the area of flourishing mixed-gender ministry partnerships. The input from participants in my study is summed up with this comment: "Communicating in a way that most people not only hear but are heard is a lot of work. It doesn't come easily; I think it's the biggest thing." Digging deeper, interviewees stressed the importance of both quantity and quality of communication.

First, quantity matters, and the consensus in the research was that abundant communication should saturate the partnership from beginning to end. As the story above illustrates, a frank conversation about topics including expectations, boundaries, and goals is a good place to start. Depending on a person's experience with mixed-gender partnership, such a conversation may be easy or, more likely, awkward. Either way, beginning a partnership with these conversations is of paramount importance.

Next, respondents pointed out the importance of ongoing debrief, which, as has been noted, is particularly important when things go wrong. One male leader cited his practice of a "conversation around a decision and then . . . a second conversation about how that conversation went." Similarly, a woman recounted her experience of joining an otherwise all-male team and finding that their communication style was "a bit locker room." When she expressed her discomfort, the team pledged to change their behavior and created a rhythm of "time-outs" following each meeting, where they could debrief any unhelpful communication dynamics that had surfaced during their time together. Rigorous debrief, either as a part of a regular rhythm or as needed, is a vital skill that individuals and communities should seek to develop.

Just as the quantity of communication throughout the partnership is important, the research attests that the quality or caliber of that communication is likewise critical. For instance, several people testified to the importance of talking about things that are often considered taboo. One supervisor noted that "effective partnership requires communication skills to talk about things like sexual tension or gender differences." Similarly, another interviewee cited the importance of having an "openness to [talking about places] where gender or race might intersect in conversation or in work you're doing. [Partners are] way better off to be talking about it than not."

Not only do flourishing mixed-gender partners talk about topics that can be difficult to talk about, they handle conflict well. In one case, a long-serving leader related the story of a persistent conflict that eventually needed intervention from a trusted third party. And in one participant observation study, I observed the woman and man who were leading the meeting having open conflict in front of their team. They were unafraid to publicly disagree, and their resolution happened publicly as well. It was clear that they had a strong partnership that could handle disagreement, and I could see how their willingness to demonstrate that level of communication would open the door to lively and vulnerable sharing around the room.

In terms of quantity and quality, then, flourishing mixed-gender ministry partnerships are marked by abundant communication. When ministry partners invest time and energy into the communication process, they are more likely to experience both higher personal satisfaction and greater missional effectiveness.

ABUNDANT COMMUNICATION IN THE BIBLE

When it comes to mixed-gender communication in the Bible, it is useful to consider how Jesus communicated with women in his day. As with just about everything related to the topic of mixed-gender ministry partnerships, Jesus was a game-changer for women in this area. In John 20:1-18, the resurrected Jesus meets Mary Magdalene in the garden outside his now-empty tomb. From this text, we can discern three insights into Jesus' practice of mixed-gender communication.[1]

First, in a day where women were systematically marginalized and largely prohibited from social interaction with men outside of their homes, Jesus treated women and men the same in his mixed-gender communication.[2] For

---

[1]A fuller treatment of Jesus' mixed-gender communication patterns and techniques would be a welcome addition to the academic literature. This interaction with Mary Magdalene will provide a basic understanding of Jesus' communication with women, but it is not meant to be seen as comprehensive.
[2]The nature of Jesus' interactions with women were on par with his interactions with men, but it is worth noting that the Gospels recount more of Jesus' conversations with men than with women.

instance, in John 20:15, he inaugurates the conversation by asking Mary two questions. He wants to know why she is weeping and whom she is looking for. Asking questions was a common communication tactic for Jesus, and he used it with men as well. For comparison, consider Jesus' interaction with John's two male disciples in John 1:35-42. In this case, he likewise begins the conversation with a question when he asks, "What are you looking for?" (John 1:38). Various commentators have remarked about Jesus' use of questions in his communication practice. Robert Stein writes, "Jesus also knew the merits of this Socratic method and frequently used questions in his teaching. He used them in a variety of ways in a variety of situations. One way was that of drawing from his audience the correct answer he sought. By drawing out the correct answer from his listeners rather than simply declaring it, Jesus impressed his point more convincingly upon their minds."[3] Asking questions is a foundational communication skill for Jesus, and he was willing to apply that skill in his interactions with both women and men.

Second, we see genuine relational affection in the communication between Jesus and Mary. For example, Jesus has only to call out her name to reveal his identity to Mary. With John 10:3-5 in view, commentator Craig Keener notes, "This fits Jesus' prior teaching: his own sheep would recognize his voice, especially when he called them by name."[4] Mary's reply to Jesus furthers this idea of relational affection. In John 20:16, she replies, calling him "Rabbouni." Though John translates this word as "Teacher" for the reader, commentator Merrill Tenney notes that that word can also be translated to something closer to "my dear Lord."[5] Jesus knows Mary's name, she knows Jesus' voice, and she considers him her dear Lord. The language Jesus and Mary use for one another in this passage is an example of the power of relational affection in the context of mixed-gender communication.

Finally, this text demonstrates Jesus' willingness to fully trust women in the context of mixed-gender communication. In the research, interviewees talked about the importance of engaging topics that are difficult to discuss, and Jesus' messianic identity would seem to fit that bill. As he does with the

---

This is one place where the Bible's Sitz im Leben comes into play; by virtue of their place in society, women would have simply had less access to Jesus than men.

[3]Robert H. Stein, *The Method and Message of Jesus' Teachings*, rev. ed. (Louisville: Westminster John Knox Press, 1994), 23. In addition to questions designed to produce self-discovery, Stein notes that Jesus also utilized counterquestions and rhetorical questions in his teaching and interactions.

[4]Craig S. Keener, *The Gospel of John: A Commentary* (Peabody, MA: Hendrickson, 2003), 2:1191.

[5]Merrill C. Tenney, *John*, Expositor's Bible Commentary (Grand Rapids, MI: Zondervan, 1981), 191.

woman at the well in John 4, Jesus once again reveals his true identity, this time to Mary (John 20:17).[6]

Further, the importance of expressing trust in communication is reinforced in the final verse in the text, as Jesus commissions Mary to communicate the truth of the resurrection to the disciples. Again, Jesus' exhortation to her to engage the disciples about his identity is noteworthy, particularly given the low esteem that a woman's testimony would carry in first-century culture and her willingness to speak given that cultural limitation likewise communicates her trust in Jesus. "Mary announces her personal-eyewitness experience even though she must be aware of the prejudice against women's testimony in her culture; she could offer it in defiance of such prejudice but most likely offers it simply because it is necessary and because she has nothing else to offer; she trusts the one who sent her to make it adequate."[7]

This brief examination of Mary's interaction with Jesus in John 20:1-18 demonstrates three dynamics present in Jesus' practice of mixed-gender communication. By asking her questions, he communicates with Mary in the same way he communicates with men; their interaction emphasizes relational affection in the communication process; and they communicate trust in their interaction with one another. Once again, Jesus serves as a model for us as we consider our own practices of mixed-gender communication.

BENEFITS OF ABUNDANT COMMUNICATION

There are at least three benefits that can come from women and men pursuing abundant communication in their ministry partnerships. For one thing, robust and effective communication can function like oil in the mixed-gender ministry partnership engine. In other words, each of the other nine attributes in the Together in Ministry model are made easier by abundant communication. For example, getting on the same theological page

---

[6]Though similar in certain respects, the experiences of the woman in John 4 and Mary in John 20 are also distinct. In John 4, Jesus clearly states his messianic identity, saying, "I am he [the Christ], the one who is speaking to you" (John 4:26). By contrast, with Mary, Jesus emphasizes his looming ascension: "I am ascending to my Father and your Father, to my God and your God" (John 20:17). The effect is the same in both cases—Jesus is revealing his true identity—but the form is different.

[7]Keener, *Gospel of John*, 2:1196. Sadly, the disciples' response to Mary's news about Jesus' resurrection seems to confirm the cultural devaluing of a woman's testimony in the sense that they require their own visitation from Jesus in order to fully embrace the truth of his resurrection. That is certainly true of Thomas, who requires physical evidence of the injuries that Jesus would have faced in the crucifixion process.

(see chap. 3) will be helped by earnest communication in the context of communal Bible study. Abundant communication would also be a necessary cornerstone of trust-filled mixed-gender friendships (see chap. 7). And developing a sensitivity to adverse gender dynamics (see chap. 8) will only be useful if the community is able to effectively communicate about what they are seeing and feeling.

Beyond this overall benefit, a second benefit is that abundant communication should get easier over time. That is, ministry partners should get better at communicating as they repeatedly push through whatever awkwardness is present. Recalling the story that began this chapter, we can assume that the twenty-fifth conversation about the status of their working partnership would be far less off-putting than the first.

In their book *Difficult Conversations*, a group of leaders from the Harvard Negotiation Project support this idea that persevering in communication can result in more effective communication. Over time and with focused effort, people can indeed move past surface-level conflict conversations to something they call a "learning conversation."[8] When people get to this point, they "come to appreciate the complexity of the perceptions and intentions involved, the reality of joint contribution to the problem, the central role feelings have to play, and what the issues mean to each person's self-esteem and identity. . . . In fact, [they] may find that [they] no longer have a message to deliver, but rather some information to share, and some questions to ask."[9] It is hard to imagine mixed-gender ministry partners communicating at this level in the beginning, but with repetition they might well get there.

Third, doing the hard work of learning how to communicate in a mixed-gender setting will be a benefit for future generations. More than once, I have noted that we lack models for how to interact naturally as women and men. It is time to break that pattern and create workable models that subsequent generations can follow. Indeed, if individuals and communities are to overcome generations of awkwardness, it is going to take courageous and intentional trailblazers to lead the way.

---

[8]The writers describe three other varieties of difficult conversations, including the "what happened" conversation, the feelings conversation, and the identity conversation. By "surface-level," I don't mean to suggest that the conversations are easy; rather, they can be quite complex. But the deeper and more productive conversation is the learning one, and that comes with practice.
[9]Douglas Stone, Bruce Patton, and Sheila Heen, *Difficult Conversations: How to Discuss What Matters Most* (New York: Penguin, 1999), 16.

BARRIERS TO ABUNDANT COMMUNICATION

Far and away, the greatest barrier to flourishing mixed-gender partnerships in this area is the clumsiness we can feel around communicating with someone of the opposite gender. More than once in the research process, an interviewee said something along the lines of "It's just awkward!"

In her appropriately titled book *Beyond Awkward Side Hugs*, Bronwyn Lea exposits the awkwardness that can be present in mixed-gender communication. In one instance, she relates a story from a mixed-gender and cross-cultural friendship where physical gestures had been misinterpreted on both sides. Following a debrief, Lea concluded, "Both of us had made physical gestures of friendship that, to the other, had been interpreted as a bid for something more. Both of us had been confused. And it was a bit awkward to talk about it. But we did, and the honest communication helped us get beyond the awkwardness and into the realm of friends-who-are-siblings."[10]

Generally speaking, mixed-gender communication is an underdeveloped skill in our communities of faith. In fact, ministry philosophies and structures often exacerbate this problem, as girls and boys, and later women and men, are often sequestered into gender-exclusive ministry spheres. One result of this separation is that we can fail to learn how to communicate in a natural way in mixed-gender settings, and so it feels awkward. Until we can normalize mixed-gender interactions in the context of ministry, our churches and organizations will continue to be saddled with an anemic capacity for mixed-gender communication.

Awkwardness is the biggest barrier to abundant mixed-gender communication, but sadly there are others. A related second barrier is our cultural bent toward silence on issues of gender. As has been noted previously, the church has spent much of its history avoiding frank conversations about gender in the hopes that not talking about what could go wrong as women and men interrelate would disempower it. The tragic reality, exposed most recently by the #MeToo and #ChurchToo movements, is that silence has not served us.[11]

---

[10]Bronwyn Lea, *Beyond Awkward Side Hugs: Living as Christian Brothers and Sisters in a Sex-Crazed World* (Nashville: Thomas Nelson, 2020), 140. As noted in chap. 1, this book does not spend much time discussing the intersection of gender, race, and other factors, but this story illustrates that often several dynamics can overlap in a given situation. This complexity would seem to call for even more focus on the attributes in this book, including abundant communication.

[11]Ruth Everhart speaks to the downsides to the church's culture of silence, specifically in the context of sexual violence. For one thing, it is good and right for survivors to share their stories as they are ready. Speaking to the importance of public lamentation, she writes, "Suppressing those cries [of

Every time I present to college students on the topic of flourishing mixed-gender ministry partnerships, I have a similar experience. The students ask question after question, and they will keep asking their questions for as long as I can stay. There is a thirst to talk about topics, such as sex and gender, that the church has long considered taboo. Young people crave these conversations, and if the church does not facilitate them, they will go somewhere that will.

A third barrier in this area can be a general lack of communication skills. My anecdotal observation is that our communication toolboxes seem to have fewer and fewer tools in them. In part, this may be a function of our dependence on screens, as a study from Elon College affirms:

> Field observations, a survey of 100 Elon students, and an analysis of previously conducted studies provided evidence that the rapid expansion of technology is negatively affecting face-to-face communication. People are becoming more reliant on communicating with friends and family through technology and are neglecting to engage personally, uninhibited by phones and devices, even when actually in the presence of others.[12]

Providing training on basic communication skills would be a worthwhile tactic for faith communities and organizations to consider.

A fourth barrier can be the question of difference in how the genders communicate with one another. One pervasive theory is that women and men communicate dramatically differently, and this idea can be a barrier to mixed-gender communication in two respects.

On one hand, this theory that women and men communicate differently relies on the notion of gender essentialism (see chap. 6). For instance, in his famous book *Men Are from Mars, Women Are from Venus*, John Gray includes what he calls a "Martian/Venusian Phrase Dictionary," a translation guide for interpreting what each gender is really saying. In one passage, Gray notes that "to fully express their feelings, women assume poetic license and use various

---

lament] is wrong. It is never faithful to silence the vulnerable, even unintentionally. This kind of silence is not sacred or useful. It does not honor survivors or the God who loves them. The noise of lamentation is sacred and useful. It sounds a warning. It creates a clamor. This is how it does its job. How else can the people of God express painful emotion, expose wrong-doing, and advocate for justice? Noise and exposure are the very gifts our society needs to receive." *The #MeToo Reckoning: Facing the Church's Complicity in Sexual Abuse and Misconduct* (Downers Grove, IL: Inter-Varsity Press, 2020), 211.

[12]Emily Drago, "The Effect of Technology on Face-to-Face Communication," *The Elon Journal of Undergraduate Research in Communications* 6, no. 1 (2015): 13-19.

superlatives, metaphors, and generalizations. Men mistakenly take these expressions literally."[13]

That framework is certainly true in some cases, but it is not in others.[14] And while Gray himself acknowledges that one size might not actually fit all when it comes to mixed-gender communication, he goes on to encourage those who don't seem to fit the stereotype to pursue deeper reflection on the premise that women and men might have "denied" or repressed standard masculine or feminine communication styles. As with the idea of gender difference more broadly, a rigid system for how the genders communicate can impede flourishing mixed-gender communication, particularly if someone defies the accepted gender stereotypes. In other words, when it comes to communication, some men are from Mars, but so are some women. Same thing for Venus. And sometimes it seems like people are actually from Saturn.

On the other hand, when the stereotypes around gendered communication differences do fit, communication can indeed be a challenge. In her work decoding stereotypical gendered communication differences, Deborah Tannen notes that "women—like people who have grown up in a different culture—have often learned different styles of speaking than men, which can make them seem less competent and self-assured than they are."[15] For Tannen, overcoming these differences requires careful consideration about how communication is both given and received.

Until we find ways to overcome these barriers of awkwardness, taboo topics, a general lack of communication skills, and the complexities embedded in the concept of gender-based communication differences, individuals and communities will continue to struggle with their mixed-gender communication.

How to Develop Abundant Mixed-Gender Communication

How can we equip individuals and communities to communicate more effectively in the context of mixed-gender ministry partnerships? To start, we would all benefit from some basic communication training. Given the realities of our

---

[13]John Gray, *Men Are from Mars, Women Are from Venus: A Practical Guide for Improving Communication and Getting What You Want in Your Relationships* (New York: HarperCollins, 1992), 60.

[14]One specific mixed-gender ministry partnership where Gray's analysis falls short is my own marriage, where the person more likely to be speaking in "superlatives, metaphors, and generalizations" is me, not my wife, Amy. Exceptions are one reason why inflexible taxonomies that purport to lay out definitive gender differences are problematic.

[15]Deborah Tannen, "The Power of Talk: Who Gets Heard and Why," in *On Women and Leadership* (Boston: Harvard Business Review Press, 2019), 68.

digital age, training on topics such as active listening, making good eye contact, and paraphrasing for understanding should become normative in our organizational settings. We should also follow Jesus' example of asking good questions, expressing affection, and communicating trust. On a personal note, I need to grow in my ability to focus in communication. I am a multitasker, and if I am not careful, I will half pay attention to someone as they are talking to me while the other half of my brain is thinking about something else entirely. I need training in how to bring my full attention to the person I am in dialogue with.

Second, this chapter started with a description of a frank conversation about expectations on the front end of a ministry partnership. This is a great place to start, but people might need help navigating such a conversation. Some time ago, the human resources director of a mission agency asked me to write some questions that women and men could consider as they begin partnering together in ministry. In response, I generated the following list:

- What is your experience working alongside someone of the opposite gender? Positive experiences? Places of struggle? What has formed you in this area? What have you learned (about yourself and about partnering with someone of the opposite gender) along the way?

- How would you characterize your theological fluency on the topic of women and men in partnership? What work have you done in the Scriptures, if any? What passages have been influential for you? Where do you still have questions?

- Do we have concerns as we enter into this partnership? Is there anything we need to process through together?

- How can we keep this partnership healthy for each one of us? What are some proactive steps we can take to make sure this is a healthy working relationship? Are there any boundaries we should consider? Who in our community can help us in this area?

- What would we like to commit to in terms of evaluating how we are doing in our ministry partnership? How often should we plan to check in about how it's going?

- As we think about working together, what are our hopes for this partnership? How can we each be praying for one another and for the partnership?

Finally, incarnating this attribute of abundant communication will require courage. As with so much in the Together in Ministry model, flourishing mixed-gender communication will not just happen. Instead, it will require courageous and intentional effort. Asked about one of the success factors in flourishing mixed-gender ministry partnerships, one interviewee captured this attribute well, reflecting on "those kinds of awkward conversations that I think require some guts, [where] we have to be honest with each other and we have to be courageous to talk about the [hard] stuff."

By focusing on general communication skills, by utilizing scripted questions, and by summoning a bit of relational courage, women and men can develop a deeper level of communication in their ministry partnerships. And, as that happens, those partnerships should flourish in greater measure.

FINAL THOUGHTS

In her seminal book about mixed-gender ministry partnerships, *Equal to the Task*, Ruth Haley Barton devotes an entire chapter to improving mixed-gender communication. She closes the chapter by recounting a story of her mixed-gender partnership with a man named Mark. Communication was difficult in Ruth and Mark's ministry partnership, but they kept working at it and finally they experienced a breakthrough. Barton writes, "At one point, after several incidents where our communication simply did not work, we finally acknowledged the difficulty and laughed about it. What a moment of freedom that was!"[16]

Abundant communication takes work, and it requires both courage and the type of grace that can yield a good laugh. The good news is that as women and men step up to the challenges of mixed-gender communication, they can experience ministry partnerships that are personally satisfying and missionally effective.

PROCESSING QUESTIONS

1. As you think about your communication toolbox, what are you consistently good at?

---

[16]Ruth Haley Barton, *Equal to the Task: Men & Women in Partnership* (Downers Grove, IL: InterVarsity Press, 1998), 112.

2. Where are you weak in interpersonal communication? What could it look like to grow in this area?

3. What barriers hold you back from communicating effectively with your mixed-gender ministry partner?

4. Are there any conversations that you have been avoiding? What would you need in order to successfully have those conversations with your ministry partner? How might the questions articulated in this chapter help you move forward in your mixed-gender communication?

10

CONTEXTUALIZED BOUNDARIES

In October of 1948, Billy Graham's ministry was just getting rolling. His rallies were starting to draw big crowds and his fame was spreading. In light of his newfound celebrity, and with an eye toward the various forces that could potentially trip up his ministry, Graham and his inner circle met in a hotel room in Modesto, California, during a series of evangelistic gatherings. There, over the course of an afternoon, they established a set of rules that would govern their ministry work, a list that came to be known as the "Modesto Manifesto."[1]

In the end, they articulated four different rules. They covenanted together to pursue scrupulous financial accountability, regular partnership with local church communities, and integrity in their publicity and reporting. Each of these rules were important to Graham and his cohort, but the fourth rule is the one that has become enshrined in churches around the world. Today this rule bears the moniker of "the Billy Graham Rule." It states that male leaders should never be alone with women who are not their wives.

Back in Modesto, the thinking was that if Billy Graham could be systematically separated from women, he would be protected from a devastating moral lapse, and no one could make a false accusation of impropriety on Graham's part. Graham himself wrote, "We all knew of evangelists who had fallen into immorality while separated from their families by travel. We pledged among ourselves to avoid any situation that would have even the appearance of

---

[1] This particular afternoon began with Graham calling his core team of Cliff Barrows, George Beverly Shea, and Grady Wilson to his hotel room to talk about how their ministry might avoid some of the pitfalls that other evangelistic ministries were facing. Graham sent each man back to his room to reflect for an hour on solutions, then brought them back together. Their lists were essentially the same, and the Modesto Manifesto was articulated. Billy Graham, "What's 'the Billy Graham Rule'?," Billy Graham Evangelistic Association, July 23, 2019, https://billygraham.org/story/the-modesto-manifesto-a-declaration-of-biblical-integrity/.

compromise or suspicion. From that day on, I did not travel, meet, or eat alone with a woman other than my wife."[2]

Over the years the Billy Graham Rule has become widely influential. Because of the Billy Graham Rule, pastors have spent decades driving separate cars to lunches and installing glass windows in their office doors, among other applications. Halee Gray Scott has conducted research regarding the Graham Rule, and she notes that "most of the men reported feeling the tension of living with integrity in a hypersexualized world. In following the Billy Graham Rule, they didn't intend to exclude women or sexualize them. Instead, they wanted to ensure their actions were always above board. They also wanted to inoculate themselves against false sexual harassment allegations."[3] Truly, for generations of leaders, the Billy Graham Rule has essentially become the Eleventh Commandment, a must-follow for every male ministry leader who aspires to have a fruitful ministry that is above proverbial reproach.[4]

But there is a problem here. Because for all the attention and energy given to the Billy Graham Rule, it hasn't proven to be a fail-safe answer to the sexual tensions embedded in the context of mixed-gender ministry partnerships. While Graham himself dodged even a hint of scandal in his decades of public life, chances are that every person reading this book knows the story of some male leader who has transgressed their personal boundaries and fallen into sin, and stories like that emerged in my study as well.

And yet it goes beyond that, because the Billy Graham Rule was also critiqued in my research as having several unintended negative consequences—stumbling blocks for women and men who would aspire to build flourishing mixed-gender ministry partnerships. So not only has Graham's rule failed to resolve the problem it was designed to address, it has also become an impediment to fully flourishing mixed-gender ministry partnerships.

THE BILLY GRAHAM RULE'S UNINTENDED CONSEQUENCES

My research revealed three examples of unintended consequences provoked by the Billy Graham Rule. First, a rigid adherence to the Billy Graham Rule

---

[2]Billy Graham, *Just as I Am: The Autobiography of Billy Graham* (New York: HarperCollins, 2018), 128.
[3]Halee Gray Scott, "To More Than a Few Good Men: Don't Give Up on Working with Women," *Christianity Today*, December 6, 2017, https://www.christianitytoday.com/ct/2017/december-web-only/dont-give-up-working-with-women-billy-graham-pence-rule.html.
[4]Interestingly, the Billy Graham Rule was broadly litigated in the run-up to the 2016 American presidential election, as then vice-presidential candidate Mike Pence turned out to be a devoted adherent to it during his time in office as the governor of Indiana.

can make it impossible for people to do their jobs. One interviewee, reflecting on her role as a supervisor tasked with developing male leaders, concluded that "I can't do my job if I can't be alone with a man." Systematically prohibiting leaders from being physically present with their followers can limit their capacity to fulfill their ministry duties.

A second consequence of a blanket acceptance of the Billy Graham Rule is that it can perpetuate the narrative that people are unable to control themselves from acting on their sexual impulses. Reflecting on just one iteration of this underlying narrative, Katelyn Beaty writes,

> The Pence rule arises from a broken view of the sexes: men are lustful beasts that must be contained, while women are objects of desire that must be hidden away. Offering the Pence rule as a solution to male predation is like saying, "I can't meet with you one on one, otherwise I might eventually assault you." If that's the case, we have far deeper problems around men and power than any personal conduct rule can solve.[5]

Several respondents decried this narrative with something akin to outrage, with one saying, "I'm a mature person, and I am in control of myself!" For these leaders, to be subjected to the Graham Rule minimizes the hard work they have done in discipleship and character formation (see chap. 4).

A third unintended consequence of the Billy Graham Rule is that it can systematically deprive women of access, power, and agency. One interviewee related the story of a time that she had to drive alone to a conference across Michigan's Upper Peninsula because a male colleague insisted on not being alone in a car with her. At one level that reality alone was painful for this woman, primarily because his decision made her feel like she was some sort of threat to him. But, at a deeper level, what was more disturbing was the lack of access the arrangement afforded her. Often the drive home from a conference is where decisions get made about what will happen with the content from the conference, and, as she put it, "women don't get the same access" when the Billy Graham Rule is in play.

These three critiques point to the harm that the Billy Graham Rule has done, primarily to women but also to men. Indeed, for the majority of those

---

[5]Katelyn Beaty, "A Christian Case Against the Pence Rule," *New York Times*, November 15, 2017, www.nytimes.com/2017/11/15/opinion/pence-rule-christian-graham.html. I have also done some reflection on the unhelpful narratives that the Graham Rule perpetuates. See Rob Dixon, "Redeeming the Stories We Tell," *Mutuality* (blog), March 4, 2016, www.cbeinternational.org/resource/article/mutuality-blog-magazine/redeeming-stories-we-tell.

surveyed, a rigid adherence to the Billy Graham Rule only hinders mixed-gender partnerships from flourishing.

A Contextualized Way Forward

Thankfully, the research process generated a viable workaround. Instead of foisting the Billy Graham Rule on every mixed-gender partnership in every setting, the research suggests that women and men should thoughtfully discern what boundaries are right for their particular partnership in light of who each person is and is becoming, and then live out those boundaries with integrity and accountability.

The issue with the Billy Graham Rule is not boundaries themselves. In fact, research participants detailed a wide assortment of usable boundaries, including meeting in public places, meeting exclusively during daytime hours, letting others know if they are traveling together, and discerning whether certain topics should be off-limits. In one instance, a veteran female leader talked about a time she and her male coworker were traveling together on a ministry trip. The trip would involve an overnight, so they decided to stay with some of her donors "because if you're in a hotel, it can look suspicious."

So, the issue for those surveyed is not the presence of boundaries; instead, it is the universal application of the supremely restrictive boundary of the Billy Graham Rule. As Danielle Strickland notes, "To create safe boundaries for your life and ministry is a good idea. But taking the ones created for a specific set of circumstances at a certain point in time for a specific person and applying them to your life and ministry today is unhelpful, and in today's world, actually harmful to women."[6] As women and men carefully discern the appropriate contextualized boundaries for their specific ministry partnership, that partnership is more likely to flourish.

The Billy Graham Rule in the Scriptures

It must be clearly stated that Jesus did not practice the Billy Graham Rule in the context of his earthly ministry. Indeed, the Billy Graham Rule is a modern stricture. One key example from Jesus' engagement with women in his day will illustrate this point.

---

[6]Danielle Strickland, *Better Together: How Women and Men Can Heal the Divide and Work Together to Transform the Future* (Nashville: Thomas Nelson, 2020), 81.

As noted previously (see chap. 2), in John 4 Jesus has a remarkable conversation with the woman at the well in which he ultimately reveals his messianic identity. The narrator, John, is careful to let the reader know that Jesus and the woman are alone as they talk. For one thing, we are told that it is "about noon" (John 4:6). This would have been an atypical time for a woman to walk to the well in order to fill up a water jug. "It was the hottest time of day, not the best time to be traveling and a very unusual time for a woman to fetch water. . . . [Women] would come to draw water at cooler periods of the day."[7]

On top of this evidence, John offers a parenthetical note that Jesus' disciples had gone into town in order to buy food (John 4:8), and indeed they return right at the end of their conversation (John 4:27). If Jesus were a committed follower of the Billy Graham Rule, wouldn't he have asked one of the Twelve to stay with him for the conversation with this woman?[8]

In this interaction, Jesus not only offends today's Billy Graham Rule, he also transgresses the cultural expectations of his day. In the first century, it would likewise have been unorthodox for a man to be alone with a woman who was not his wife. In his book *The Powers That Be*, theologian Walter Wink notes that "Jesus violated the mores of his time in every single encounter with women recorded in the four Gospels."[9] That observation is certainly true with respect to the Billy Graham Rule, both in the first century as well as today.

BENEFITS OF CONTEXTUALIZED BOUNDARIES

Taking a contextualized approach to boundaries in the context of mixed-gender ministry partnerships offers at least three advantages. To begin with, opting for a contextualized approach can free women from the effects of the

---

[7]Rodney A. Whitacre, *John* (Downers Grove, IL: InterVarsity Press, 1999), 101. Whitacre makes the assessment that the woman's decision to collect water at this awkward time must be the result of her scandalous reputation in the community. Citing the textual note about this woman's involvement with six different men, Whitacre makes the evaluation that she would be avoiding the town's women due to her adulterous ways. It is worth noting that there are other rationales for why this woman had been involved with these many men, including the possibilities that she had been repeatedly divorced or widowed. This alternate understanding gains momentum with how the passage ends, as she goes into town and successfully introduces the community to Jesus. Would that have happened if she were a social pariah? Reflecting on the spiritual impact of the woman at the well, Kamila Blessing notes that "in a powerful way, one that defies social convention, she carries out the functions of a true disciple." "John," in *The IVP Women's Bible Commentary* (Downers Grove, IL: InterVarsity Press, 2002), 598.
[8]In today's church, when we think about the Billy Graham Rule, we envision confined spaces, such as an office or car. The well at Sychar would have been a public environment, but in the first-century context the comparison stands. For Jesus to be alone with this woman would have been socially inappropriate, and yet that does not stop him from engaging the woman in conversation.
[9]Walter Wink, *The Powers That Be: Theology for a New Millennium* (New York: Doubleday, 1999), 129.

unintended consequences mentioned above. Specifically, a set of boundaries tailored to a particular mixed-gender ministry partnership can allow women to express the full scope of their jobs; it can overwrite the unhelpful narratives that undergird the Billy Graham Rule; and it can affirm a woman's power and agency. Our faith communities desperately need female leaders who are empowered to fulfill their ministry callings, and freedom from the unintended shackles of the Billy Graham Rule is one way to help that happen.

A second benefit to pursuing this type of contextualized boundary framework lies in the very nature of contextualization itself. When something is contextualized it is designed to fit a certain situation or circumstance. Because of this, a contextualized alternative generally functions better than a standardized or universal one. During the research process, it became clear over time that no two mixed-gender ministry partnerships are alike. They vary in plenty of ways, including duration, proximity, maturity, power dynamics, and more. A contextualized approach permits both partners to carefully discern what would be healthy for them. Contextualized boundaries are flexible, and that flexibility allows them to change as the partnership develops over time as well.

A third benefit to adopting a contextualized approach to boundaries in mixed-gender ministry partnerships is that it can shift the focus from following rules to developing character. In a Vox essay, university professor Karen Swallow Prior notes that "good character is even more trustworthy than the most well-intentioned rules."[10] Further, she prescribes the virtue of prudence, "the virtue most applicable in the context of guarding against workplace romances, the habit of making right decisions. Prudence, which literally means foresight, is the mean between cunning and negligence. It is wisdom in action." In flourishing mixed-gender ministry partnerships, character and virtue formation should be the priority, with an emphasis on helping individuals move toward healing and wholeness in the areas of gender brokenness in their lives. Appropriate boundaries should flow from that process, as opposed to directing it.

BARRIERS TO CONTEXTUALIZED BOUNDARIES

There are significant benefits to adopting a contextualized approach to boundaries in mixed-gender ministry partnerships, but likewise there are significant

---

[10]Karen Swallow Prior, "The Problem with 'Don't Eat Alone with Women': Good Character Is Better Than Strict Rules," *Vox*, April 1, 2017, www.vox.com/platform/amp/first-person/2017 /4/1/15142744/mike-pence-billy-graham-rule.

barriers. First and foremost, as noted above, the Billy Graham Rule is the established guideline in churches and faith communities around the world. It is standard operating procedure for millions of leaders. Because of this, a fresh approach to managing boundaries will encounter the built-in resistance of precedence.

In fact, we have seen these dynamics in play in the response of many churches and leaders to the #MeToo and #ChurchToo movements. Writing in 2018, Thom Rainer, a prominent evangelical leader, predicted that one response to #MeToo would be a fresh embrace of the Billy Graham Rule: "The Billy Graham rule, at its essence, says a person should not be alone with a person of the opposite gender if that person is not your spouse. This practice, disparaged and ridiculed by many as archaic, legalistic, and unfair, could have saved a lot of heartache if it had been embraced earlier. It will bring changes in counseling, travel, and meetings."[11] Any rule can and will be circumvented, including the Billy Graham Rule, but that hasn't stopped leaders like Rainer for calling for a recommitment to it in light of this cultural moment.

Second, not only is the Billy Graham Rule considered settled policy, it remains firmly held in place by fear. Too many pastors and leaders live in fear of what might happen with a sexual misstep, or they live in fear of what others might assume should they be seen with someone who is not their spouse. In the same way that fear can inhibit the formation of mixed-gender friendships (see chap. 7), fear can also impede efforts to adopt a fresh model of contextualized boundaries.

Recently, I was conducting training on the Together in Ministry model, and we hosted a breakout session for men, for the purpose of talking about rethinking the Billy Graham Rule. Most of the men in the circle were open to the idea, but one pastor simply could not go there with us. Instead, he was insistent that a rigid Billy Graham Rule policy was the only godly way to go. When I asked him why he thought that, he said, "I know too many good pastors who have fallen, and I'm afraid of that happening to me."

Sexual transgressions are real. They happen. This pastor's fear was legitimate.[12] The issue was not that he was afraid; it was that he was bound by his

---

[11]Thom S. Rainer, "Five Ways the #MeToo Movement Will Likely Impact Churches," *Church Answers*, August 13, 2018, https://thomrainer.com/2018/08/five-ways-metoo-movement-will-likely -impact-churches/.

[12]Reliable statistics on this are difficult to find, but the anecdotal evidence is certainly strong. As I am writing this chapter, news has broken of a famous Hillsong pastor who has admitted to being

fear, and he was unable or unwilling to look beyond it. The Gospels remind us that it is possible to have fear and yet respond in faith.[13] Contextualized boundaries coupled with accountability can be one way to move ahead with faith over fear in this area.

A third barrier to embracing a framework of contextualized boundaries for mixed-gender ministry partnerships is that doing so requires an honest self-assessment (see chap. 4). Doing that inner work, confronting our sin and brokenness around gender, requires a level of maturity and intentionality that not enough of us have. Instead, as Eugene Peterson points out,

> Millions of people in our culture make decisions for Christ, but there is a dreadful attrition rate. Many claim to have been born again, but the evidence for mature Christian discipleship is slim. . . . There is a great market for religious experience in our world; there is little enthusiasm for the patient acquisition of virtue, little inclination to sign up for a long apprenticeship in what earlier generations of Christians called holiness.[14]

Contextualized boundaries will require an unflinching examination of our inner lives around gender brokenness. In the words of Psalm 51:6, we will need to understand what is really happening in our "secret heart." If we are unable to identify and examine our gender brokenness, we won't be able to make right decisions about the boundaries that will work best for us.

Fourth, an honest assessment of gender brokenness must be paired with an equally honest conversation with our ministry partner—a conversation that will require courage. We do not have enough models for talking about our brokenness, and gender brokenness in particular, with people of our own gender, much less people of the opposite gender. And yet a conversation at that level is required.

Finally, adopting a model of contextualized boundaries will require attentive accountability and support. By its nature, a one-size-fits-all rule such as the Billy Graham Rule is easier to monitor. A person is either with someone

---

unfaithful in his marriage. Whether or not people personally know clergy who have fallen, they undoubtedly know stories that demonstrate this reality.

[13]Jesus discusses this idea in multiple places, but one example comes in Mark 4:35-41. On the lake and facing a violent storm, the disciples panic and beg for Jesus' help. After miraculously calming the sea, he looks at them and says, "Why are you afraid? Have you still no faith?"

[14]Eugene Peterson, *A Long Obedience in the Same Direction: Discipleship in an Instant Society,* 20th anniv. ed. (Downers Grove, IL: InterVarsity Press, 2000), 16.

from the opposite gender who is not their spouse, or they are not. The Billy Graham Rule is black and white. Contextualized boundaries are not quite as simple. They require nuance, and they therefore necessitate individualized support and accountability. It can be difficult to find an accountability partner who has the vision and bandwidth to oversee a contextualized set of boundaries in a mixed-gender ministry partnership.

These five barriers are daunting. The road toward contextualized boundaries will not be easy. But it will be worth it, as contextualized boundaries empower individuals and communities to build flourishing mixed-gender ministry partnerships in greater measure.

How to Embrace Contextualized Boundaries

Instead of a blanket embrace of the Billy Graham Rule, would-be mixed-gender ministry partners can take the following steps in discerning, articulating, and then living out a contextualized set of thoughtful boundaries. First, in alignment with the self-awareness attribute (see chap. 4), each person should have a clear picture of what would be healthy or wise for themselves. Given someone's particular history or development, more restrictive boundaries might be necessary, or perhaps not.

Next, partners should pursue an earnest conversation about what would be wise, given where each are at on their journeys. More than likely, conversations like these will be foreign to us, so people might experience some level of awkwardness. We will need to employ all the communication skills discussed in chapter nine. In addition, multiple conversations might be necessary in order to arrive at a clear picture of what thoughtful boundaries could entail in context.

Third, bringing decisions about contextualized boundaries into the context of community would be a helpful next step. In her book *Pursuing God's Will Together*, Ruth Haley Barton articulates the importance of community in the development of individuals. She writes, "We are also committed to being a transforming community—making sure that our life together has a transforming effect on the individuals involved."[15] Accountability is one way to express Barton's vision. Selecting people who can regularly check in on a partnership's agreed-on boundaries would be a wise move.

---

[15]Ruth Haley Barton, *Pursuing God's Will Together: A Discernment Practice for Leadership Groups* (Downers Grove, IL: InterVarsity Press, 2012), 98.

That is particularly true if individuals in the partnership start to develop romantic feelings.[16]

Finally, mixed-gender ministry partners should plan to check in regularly about the boundaries they have set for themselves. Having a weekly or monthly rhythm can ensure that boundaries are followed and that they continue to be the right boundaries for that particular partnership. Some questions that could be useful in a regular check in could include:

- How are we feeling about this conversation about our boundaries? Do we have any concerns that we should process through?

- Have either of us been tempted to transgress our boundaries since we last checked in?

- How are the boundaries that we've committed to working for us right now? Do we need to make any tweaks or modifications?

- How are our contextualized boundaries helping us to flourish?

- How is our accountability system working? Are we receiving the support we need as we continue to pursue a flourishing partnership?

As with every attribute in this model for flourishing mixed-gender ministry partnerships, these action steps will require intentional effort and courage. Rethinking our traditional approach to boundaries in the context of our mixed-gender ministry partnerships will not be easy, but it will be worth it.

FINAL THOUGHTS

Several years ago, Anglican priest Tish Harrison Warren wrote an open letter on InterVarsity's blog *The Well*. In the letter, Warren thanks the men in her life who have willfully broken the Billy Graham Rule as a part of their leadership and siblingship in her life. The list of those mentioned includes college pastors, seminary professors, ministry supervisors, and various friends and colleagues.

---

[16]People often ask me about what happens if individuals in a mixed-gender ministry partnership develop romantic feelings for the other person. To begin with, we shouldn't be surprised if this happens; after all, ministry partners often spend plenty of time together, and there can be something very compelling and attractive about watching another person use their gifts in the ministry context. Sometimes one person has feelings, other times both partners develop feelings for one another. If feelings develop, my encouragement is to push through whatever awkwardness is present to talk about what is happening, with third-party help if needed. Once the feelings are out on the table, the partners can discern appropriate next steps, which could include continuing or discontinuing the ministry partnership.

To these men, Warren writes:

You, men-who've-met-with-me-one-on-one, who've eaten with me, had coffee with me, mentored me, encouraged me, and befriended me—you have changed my life. I am a Christian because you poured into me. I am a pastor because you pastored me. I am, I hope, a better wife and mother because you are in my life.

You did not see me as a sexual threat to be avoided, but as a human being, even a sister. And you were safe. You never hit on me. You never made me feel weird or uneasy. If you ever struggled with sexual temptation, you've dealt with that by talking with your wife, male friends, or a counselor so that you could be a friend, brother, and pastor to women around you. Because of that, I have the gift of having men in my life who are trustworthy and who are true, dear friends.

I am grateful to you, my brothers and pastors. Thank you for talking to me about theology and politics—because you didn't assume women don't care about these topics or aren't smart enough to engage them. Thank you for not hiving yourself off at parties, with the men in one room and the women in another. Thank you for breaking the "Billy Graham rule," for not winking at subtle sexism in the name of propriety, and for caring about me more than you clung to legalism and fear. Thank you for seeing me as someone worthy of love and investment, and not simply as a temptation to avoid. Mostly, I thank you for seeing me as a human being, God's image bearer, who, like you, needs Jesus and pastors and friends and good conversation over coffee.[17]

The Billy Graham Rule worked well for Billy Graham in his time, place, and circumstances. And while it has no doubt benefited others in the years since Modesto, it is past time to reckon with the more than seventy years of unhelpful consequences. Not only has the Billy Graham Rule failed to fully fix the problems it was designed to solve, its unintended consequences have actually brought oppression and pain, particularly for women in our ministry contexts. Therefore, it is time to forgo a blanket adherence to the Billy Graham Rule. Instead, women and men should be thoughtful and contextual in their conversations about boundaries, deciding what works for them and moving forward with integrity and accountability. As we do so, may we see greater flourishing in the mixed-gender ministry partnerships in our contexts.

---

[17]Tish Harrison Warren, "An Open Letter to Men Who Broke the Billy Graham Rule," *The Well* (blog), April 4, 2017, https://thewell.intervarsity.org/blog/open-letter-men-who-broke-billy -graham-rule.

Processing Questions

1. What have your experiences been with the Billy Graham Rule? How has it been helpful? How might it have been harmful?

2. As you consider the mixed-gender ministry partnerships that you have been a part of, what are some boundaries that have worked for you?

3. What would you need in order to have a conversation about boundaries with a partner in your ministry context? What could such a conversation entail?

4. As you establish and work within contextualized boundaries in a mixed-gender ministry partnership you are a part of, what could accountability look like for you and your ministry partner?

11

PUBLIC AFFIRMATION AND MODELING

During his interview, one participant told me about a time he had shared a preaching assignment with one of his female ministry partners. It was in a conference setting, and he and his partner stood together on stage in front of an auditorium full of college students. Reflecting on the experience, he remembered how when it was no longer his turn to speak, he would stand to the side, ceding the pulpit to his ministry partner. Following his step to the side, he would turn and face the woman who was now doing the preaching.

I was intrigued by his story because of my personal experience in situations like this one. When I am no longer the one on the microphone, I also step to the side, but then I scour my notes, preparing my heart and mind for my next turn at the microphone. Then, with whatever mental bandwidth I have left, I listen to my colleague as she preaches.

When I expressed my wonder at this leader's discipline in standing to the side and devoting his full attention to his co-presenter, he told me that he was trying to accomplish two objectives. First, he wanted to listen carefully to his partner so that his forthcoming words would integrate well. Next, by choosing to stand and face his colleague with his full attention, he was seeking to demonstrate what it looks like to sit under the teaching authority of a woman.

What a compelling picture of flourishing mixed-gender ministry partnerships! More to the point, this happened publicly, in front a roomful of students. And while we have no way of knowing how many of them even noticed what was happening on stage that day, perhaps some of them did. When individuals and communities take intentional steps to demonstrate their value for mixed-gender ministry partnerships, either through public affirmation or modeling, partnerships are more likely to flourish.

MODELING AND PUBLIC AFFIRMATION IN THE RESEARCH

About half of those surveyed cited this attribute as integral to forming flourishing mixed-gender ministry partnerships. To be specific, respondents pointed out two aspects: modeling and public affirmation, either through verbal proclamation or purposeful representation.

Modeling is important in any community or organization, in part because it gives younger members a vision for how to develop as leaders, as well as how to function successfully in the community culture. In *The Making of a Leader*, Dr. Bobby Clinton cites the importance of Margaret Barber's modeling in the development of Chinese missionary Watchman Nee. He notes, "Her wise counsel, knowledge of the Scriptures, and submissive spirit deeply affected [Nee] at an impressionable stage of his development."[1] In other words, it wasn't just Barber's words that God used to shape Nee; it was also her modeled actions.

This principle was reinforced in the research. At one point, I separately interviewed both halves of a mixed-gender ministry partnership. When I asked them about what motivated them to work closely together in ministry, they each pointed to three different mixed-gender ministry partnerships above them on the organizational chart. As we continued to talk about their experience, they noted that having those models gave them permission to try mixed-gender ministry partnership out for themselves and that they had available resources if they needed support.

Similarly, a veteran leader sounded a bit of a warning in this area: "Even though [people] might believe in equality and partnership, the ability to practice [mixed-gender partnerships] instinctively can be hampered by a lack of models and experience." Models matter, particularly when individuals and communities are stepping out into new territory.

Alongside modeling, interviewees pointed to the importance of public affirmation in inculcating and reinforcing the value for flourishing mixed-gender ministry partnerships, especially in an organizational or communal setting. In their interviews, respondents divided this idea of public affirmation into two categories: verbal proclamation of the value of mixed-gender ministry partnerships and purposeful representation.

As with modeling, verbal proclamation can provide a permission structure for women and men to try out mixed-gender partnerships in their ministry

---

[1] J. Robert Clinton, *The Making of a Leader: Recognizing the Lessons and Stages of Leadership Development*, 2nd ed. (Colorado Springs: NavPress, 2012), 114.

contexts. For instance, one supervisor talked about "highlighting partnerships that really work well and celebrating them widely." Similarly, others related stories of when their leaders publicly honored their efforts to partner together as women and men in ministry. The intentional practice of verbally affirming a community's value for mixed-gender ministry partnerships can spur individuals into action in their particular ministry contexts.

Alongside verbal proclamation, flourishing mixed-gender ministry partnerships benefit from purposeful and public representation. When the value for flourishing mixed-gender ministry partnerships finds expression in public structures, mixed-gender partnerships can be formed and strengthened. Many people testified to the notion that representation requires intentionality.

For instance, one interviewee noted her teams' practice of asking, "Who is leading up front, and who is not yet being represented?" Habitually asking this question ensured that they were making proactive decisions about gender representation, as well as other forms of representation, which enabled them to publicly affirm their vision and values. Others noted practices such as purposefully choosing women to exposit the Scriptures; cospeaking arrangements where women and men teach or train in partnership; and shared emcee roles with both genders represented.[2]

When individuals and communities choose to consciously affirm their value and practice of mixed-gender ministry partnerships, flourishing partnerships are more likely to become normative throughout the community. Modeling and public affirmation each have a part to play in the establishment of flourishing mixed-gender ministry partnerships.

PUBLIC AFFIRMATION AND MODELING IN THE SCRIPTURES

We see this same impulse toward public affirmation and modeling in the Scriptures, most notably in the ministry of the apostle Paul. Just about everything was public in the apostle Paul's ministry among the churches. Paul shared in detail about his personal struggles[3] and his dreams for his future,[4] and he calls

---

[2]Representation matters, but so does putting qualified people into ministry roles. Ideally, individuals and communities will have a robust and diverse roster of qualified ministers to choose from in discerning who should be empowered into various ministry roles. With such a roster in place, issues of representation can take center stage.

[3]The passage in 2 Corinthians 11:16-33 details a lengthy list of Paul's travails, including imprisonments, floggings, a shipwreck, bandits, sleeplessness, and hunger.

[4]Paul sounds an almost wistful tone in 2 Timothy 4:6-8 as he expresses his hope for the "crown of righteousness" that awaits him in heaven.

out those who have persecuted him.[5] Though there were seasons when Paul was more removed from public life, while he was active in ministry, Paul's life was fundamentally a public one.

With this in mind, and understanding Paul's positive perspective on women and men in partnership (see chap. 3), it is no surprise that Paul's repeated pattern was to demonstrate his commitment to mixed-gender ministry partnerships. We see this in his choices to both model and publicly affirm his commitment in his ministry among the churches.

For one thing, Paul made no secret of the partnerships he developed with women in his ministry networks. Again, in an era where women were routinely and systematically denied access to leadership roles outside of the home, Paul's practice was to partner out in the open. As has been noted in previous chapters, the list of women who partnered with Paul in the work of the gospel is a long one and includes no fewer than eighteen women.[6] Paul was continually modeling mixed-gender ministry partnerships, and he was famous for inviting his disciples to follow his example. Indeed, in Philippians 3:17, he writes, "Join in imitating me, and observe those who live according to the example you have in us." Imitating Paul would, among other things, clearly mean practicing mixed-gender ministry partnerships.

But Paul's public affirmation of his value for mixed-gender ministry partnerships didn't stop with modeling. It extended into the realm of proclamation as well. Most notably we see this in Paul's foundational egalitarian statement in Galatians 3:28, but we also find it in more subtle places. For example, consider the final chapter of Philippians, where Paul uses precious space in his letter to invite two women to get along. In Philippians 4:2-3, Paul writes, "I urge Euodia and I urge Syntyche to be of the same mind in the Lord. Yes, and I ask you also, my loyal companion, help these women, for they have struggled beside me in the work of the gospel, together with Clement and the rest of my co-workers, whose names are in the book of life."

As mentioned in chapter eight when discussing Phoebe's role with the letter to the church in Rome, letters like this one would be read aloud to the entire congregation. In fact, Paul himself calls for this practice in

---

[5]There are many examples where Paul publicly calls out those who have opposed him. For instance, in 2 Timothy 1:15 Paul reminds his protégé that "all who are in Asia have turned away from me, including Phygelus and Hermogenes."

[6]Marg Mowczko, "Paul and Women, in a Nutshell," blog, October 6, 2014, https://margmowczko.com/paul-and-women-in-a-nutshell/.

1 Thessalonians 5:27. And so we might imagine the chagrin that these two women would have felt as they heard their names read and their quarrel publicly aired.

And yet Paul's choice to publicly call out their feud makes sense, given at least three factors. First, these two women clearly matter to Paul. Their disagreement irks Paul to the point where he takes the step of publicly naming them. Gordon Fee writes, "It is hard for us to sense how extraordinary this moment is. Apart from greetings and the occasional mention of his coworkers or envoys, Paul rarely ever mentions anyone by name. But here he does, and not because Euodia and Syntyche are the 'bad ones' who need to be singled out—precisely the opposite. That he names them at all is evidence of friendship, since one of the marks of enmity in polemical letters is that enemies are left unnamed, thus denigrated by anonymity."[7] The intentional and unconventional choice to call out Euodia and Syntyche for their feud in this public letter reflects how much Paul values them as friends and ministry partners.

Second, in Paul's view these women clearly matter to the mission. They have struggled alongside Paul, they have done the work of the gospel, and, because of their service, their names are secure in the book of life. In fact, such is the importance of their ministry that an unnamed leader in the church is instructed to step in to referee their dispute. The primary issue in the letter to the Philippians is a lack of unity, a problem that threatens to limit the church's gospel mission, and that disunity is exemplified by this relational conflict. For Paul, if a unified and reconciled Euodia and Syntyche can be useful in restoring unity and expanding God's mission, some degree of public discomfort is worth it.

Third, Paul's conviction that women and men belong in flourishing mixed-gender ministry partnerships is solid enough to warrant a potential public shaming. Reflecting on the implications of this passage, Fred B. Craddock writes, "For all the dispute about Paul's attitude toward women, they are very visibly and significantly present in his references to associates in ministry."[8] Paul's theology and practice around mixed-gender ministry partnerships were already known to the community, so why not call out these female partners for their dispute?

---

[7]Gordon Fee, *Philippians*, IVP New Testament Commentary Series (Downers Grove, IL: InterVarsity Press, 1999), 167.
[8]Fred B. Craddock, *Philippians*, Interpretation (Atlanta: John Knox, 1985), 71.

Time and again, Paul's vigorous affirmation of his value for flourishing mixed-gender ministry partnerships is manifest in both his modeling and his public affirmation. As individuals and communities pursue flourishing mixed-gender ministry partnerships, they would do well to emulate Paul's example.

BENEFITS OF PUBLIC AFFIRMATION AND MODELING

There are at least two benefits that come with modeling and publicly affirming mixed-gender ministry partnerships. Perhaps the most significant benefit is permission. When individuals and communities can see and hear about models around them, they are more likely to adopt those models for themselves.

I am writing this chapter in the midst of a national conversation about wearing face masks in public as a way to slow the spread of the coronavirus pandemic. The vast majority of Americans are committed mask wearers,[9] and yet there are a vocal minority who are not. Who is giving this minority group permission to not wear face masks? In part, it is elected officials, including the president, choosing not to model the wearing of masks in public. As one person said, "I mean, if [the president is] not wearing a mask, I'm not going to wear a mask. If he's not worried, I'm not worried."[10] Modeling is a powerful thing, in part because it extends permission—for good or for ill.

A second benefit to making public choices to model and publicly affirm a value for mixed-gender ministry partnerships is the possibility of influencing others to likewise embrace this value and practice. The choice to broadcast our values, then, could have an exponential effect, inviting women and men in our communities to enter into partnerships that bring greater personal satisfaction and missional effectiveness.

In chapter three, I mentioned how my staff partner Tina and I host periodic seminars for college students designed to help them think through their theology around women in leadership and mixed-gender ministry partnership. While we hope and trust that the seminar content shapes their

---

[9]According to one article from May 2020, 84 percent of Americans admitted to wearing a mask in public in an effort to slow the spread of the virus. Rebecca Morin, "Wear A Mask in Public? Sure. Majority of Democrats, Republicans Say They Have, Survey Shows," USA Today, May 25, 2020, www.usatoday.com/story/news/politics/2020/05/21/coronavirus-wearing-mask-public -common-nationscape-survey-finds/5215365002/.

[10]Chris Cillizza, "Donald Trump's Anti-Mask Campaign Picks Up Steam," The Point, CNN Politics, May 26, 2020, www.cnn.com/2020/05/26/politics/donald-trump-mask-joe-biden/index.html.

perspectives, we are also convinced that our example will do so as well. Our intention is to influence the students by example, alongside their theological exploration.

BARRIERS TO PUBLIC AFFIRMATION AND MODELING

At the core of this particular attribute is a choice to publicly live out and proclaim a value of mixed-gender ministry partnerships. Unfortunately, there are at least three barriers that could inhibit individuals and communities from making this choice.

One barrier could be a lack of conviction. Failing to choose to publicly demonstrate this value can reveal a half-hearted approach to the idea of mixed-gender ministry partnerships. To have integrity, individuals and communities should only seek to model and publicly affirm this value if they hold it at the level of conviction (see chap. 3).

Second, we can get so caught up doing our ministry work that we fail to ask the bigger-picture questions of representation and proclamation. Unless we stop and make space to reflect on what is happening, we can fail to make proactive choices about how we do our work.

In their seminal work on change dynamics, Heifetz and Linsky introduce the concepts of the dance floor and the balcony. In their framework, the dance floor equates to the day-in, day-out work that people are engaged in. In the context of this book, that is the work of ministry. The balcony represents the bigger-picture view, as leaders are able to look down at the dance floor to ask deeper questions about what is happening and why. For Heifetz and Linsky, successful leaders "move back and forth between the dance floor and the balcony, making interventions, observing their impact in real time, and then returning to the action."[11] It can be difficult to pay attention to the bigger issues of proclamation and representation when one is exclusively engaged on the dance floor.

At one point in my ministry life, I was coteaching with my ministry partner Tina on the topic of gender reconciliation. I was excited to speak on that topic with Tina in large part because we would be literally practicing what we were preaching. We worked hard to prepare our talk and then stood up in front of a roomful of people to present. As it turned out, we had a pastor friend in the

---

[11]Ronald A. Heifetz and Marty Linsky, *Leadership on the Line: Staying Alive through the Dangers of Leading* (Boston, MA: Harvard Business Review Press, 2002), 53.

crowd that day, and when we were finished, he came up to share his experience with us. He had a lot of great things to say about our talk, but he also had some hard news for me. He had timed it on his watch and found that I had spoken for roughly two-thirds of the total time of our talk. I couldn't believe it, but on further reflection, I knew he was right. In my zeal to present on a topic I was passionate about, I had steamrolled Tina and dominated the speaking time— ironically in a talk about gender reconciliation!

Sometimes, we can simply lose track of what is happening around us on the dance floor. Unless we make space to get up on the balcony and consider the bigger-picture questions, we may miss opportunities to represent and embody our value for flourishing mixed-gender ministry partnerships.

A third barrier to publicly affirming and modeling this value for mixed-gender ministry partnerships is the potential for pushback. Anytime we do things publicly, we run the risk of people disagreeing with our values or approach. In Paul's ministry, public pushback was a constant reality. While there are no stories in the Bible of pushback specifically because of Paul's theology and practice regarding flourishing mixed-gender ministry partnerships, we can surmise that more than a few eyebrows were raised during his ministry among the churches.

Some years ago, one of my female ministry partners was preaching at our weekly fellowship meeting, in alignment with our egalitarian conviction that women are invited by God to use their gifts in all ministry contexts. During her sermon, several men appeared at the entrance to the lecture hall. Pastors from a nearby congregation had come to investigate whether or not our Inter-Varsity community was really permitting women to preach the Scriptures. When they observed that this was indeed our practice, they proceeded to pull their financial support for our ministry. Being faithful to our convictions came with a cost, but it was one we were willing to pay. When individuals and communities make the choice to publicly display their value for flourishing mixed-gender ministry partnerships, they may well have to endure some degree of pushback.

PUBLICLY MODELING AND AFFIRMING THIS VALUE

Going public with a value for flourishing mixed-gender ministry partnerships can happen as individuals and communities take the following three steps. First, people would do well to make sure that their value for flourishing mixed-gender ministry partnerships is authentically held, that it is a conviction and not something they are pursuing simply to make themselves look better. Unfortunately, we live in a world that knows the reality of hypocrisy. Please do not seek to model something you are not committed to embodying.

Second, individuals and communities should be on the lookout for success stories that can be shared and profiled. In their book *Switch*, Chip and Dan Heath point out the value of locating and then broadcasting bright spots, "successful efforts worth emulating."[12] Bright spots are important because they demonstrate the efficacy of a value or idea. Sounding an emphatic note, the Heath brothers exhort individuals and communities to build on bright spots: "Anytime you have a bright spot, your mission is to clone it."[13] Making it a priority to share mixed-gender ministry partnership success stories in your organization can go a long way to shaping a positive culture in this area.

Third, individuals and communities should make space to seriously consider issues of representation. What a community chooses to put out for public consumption communicates its values. Some questions that might be helpful to consider include:[14]

- Who is up front in your regular community meetings or services?

- What pictures are you posting on your websites and other promotional materials?

- What is the gender composition of your leadership team?

- What stories are you telling to illustrate what God is doing in your community, and do they illustrate your value for flourishing mixed-gender partnerships?

- When it comes to the high-profile ministry opportunities in the life of your community—such as preaching, casting vision, making decisions—who is at the helm?[15]

---

[12]Chip Heath and Dan Heath, *Switch: How to Change Things When Change is Hard* (New York: Broadway, 2010), 28.

[13]Heath and Heath, *Switch*, 43.

[14]Questions like these would of course also be useful to considering other aspects of representation, including ethnic/racial diversity.

[15]In Hollywood, the Bechdel Test is used to quantify female representation in a movie. To pass the Bechdel Test, a movie must have at least two named female characters who have a conversation with one another about anything other than a man. The goal of the Bechdel Test is to ensure the representation of active female characters on screen. Danielle Strickland proposes that organizations and communities create their own version of the Bechdel Test. Perhaps the questions above

FINAL THOUGHTS

When I got to college, I was unsure if I wanted to continue on with what I viewed as my family's faith, and I spent the first several months of my time at school trying to sort that out. Ultimately, I got involved in an InterVarsity Bible study that met in my residence hall. As was typical in our InterVarsity community, that Bible study was co-led by a mixed-gender team of students, Daisy and Dave.

As I reflect on that experience, it is easy to see how it formed me. In Daisy and Dave's example, mixed-gender ministry partnerships were normalized for me early on, and that experience was reinforced time and again during my time in our community. In fact, those experiences have become the foundation for what my ministry has become, including the writing of this book. Daisy and Dave—and so many others—thank you for publicly affirming and modeling your value for flourishing mixed-gender ministry partnerships.

PROCESSING QUESTIONS

1. How has the value of mixed-gender ministry partnerships been modeled for you? Who have you learned from about how to effectively partner together with someone of the opposite gender?

2. What could it look like for you to proactively model flourishing mixed-gender ministry partnerships for others in your community or organization?

3. Give your community a letter grade for its public representation of mixed-gender ministry partnerships. Why that grade?

4. What can you and your community do to more purposefully represent and proclaim your value for mixed-gender ministry partnerships?

---

can help make that a reality. *Better Together: How Women and Men Can Heal the Divide and Work Together to Transform the Future* (Nashville: Thomas Nelson, 2020), 85.

CONCLUSION

Together in Ministry

FOR MY RESEARCH PROCESS, I EMPLOYED a philosophical framework known as Appreciative Inquiry. This approach invites research participants to reflect on when things have gone well or to dream about how they might go well in the future. "Appreciative Inquiry provides an organization-wide mode for initiating and discerning narratives and practices that are generative (creative and life giving)."[1] In this way, Appreciative Inquiry brings a hopeful posture to the research process.[2]

Consistent with an Appreciative Inquiry philosophy, I concluded each of my interviews with a question that invited participants to express their dreams for what flourishing mixed-gender partnerships could look like in practice in InterVarsity. To be specific, I asked the following question: "If you had three wishes for mixed-gender ministry partnerships throughout InterVarsity, or your part of InterVarsity, what would they be?" The inspiring responses to this question depict mixed-gender ministry partnerships that are indeed personally satisfying and missionally effective.

For instance, many envisioned a day where all InterVarsity staff would be proficient at mixed-gender ministry partnerships. One interviewee said, "What if the staff experience was, 'Oh look, we can actually work together like normal people?'" Another remarked, "My dream is that every InterVarsity staff would build a deep friendship with someone from the opposite gender." And

---

[1]Mark Lau Branson, *Memories, Hopes, and Conversations: Appreciative Inquiry and Congregational Change* (Lanham, MD: Rowman & Littlefield, 2004), 19. Branson's book takes the Appreciative Inquiry approach and demonstrates its efficacy in the context of congregational change.
[2]The weakness of the Appreciative Inquiry approach is its lack of explicit critique. To mitigate this weakness, I included an evaluative question in my interview list, and if respondents wanted to offer critique, I was happy to listen. Still, my dominant research posture was framed by Appreciative Inquiry, and it seemed to make the process enjoyable for everyone.

yet another person replied, "What if [mixed-gender ministry partnerships] became the bread and butter of who we are and how we do our work?"

Next, respondents noted that flourishing mixed-gender ministry partnerships would mean that both women and men were truly thriving. This could include women "living into who they are," "finding their voices early on during their time with InterVarsity," and "having a seat at the table even during the 'baby years.'" For men, this could mean "empowering their female staff partners," "making space for women to take their rightful seats at the table," and "increasing in self-awareness about their privilege."

Lastly, interviewees dreamed about how InterVarsity's systems and culture could more fully endorse and empower flourishing mixed-gender ministry partnerships. One leader envisioned a day when "every woman in InterVarsity would feel like there isn't a glass ceiling." Others imagined more women at higher leadership levels, salary equity between women and men, and a "more robust and shared theology about sexuality and gender."

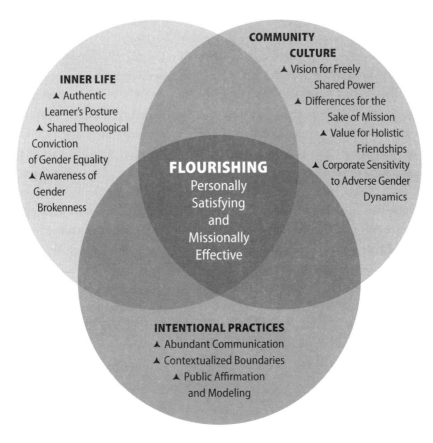

GETTING THERE

The Together in Ministry model, with its ten attributes of ministry partnerships grouped into the three larger domains of inner life, community culture, and intentional practices, is one way for individuals and communities to make these visions for a flourishing future a reality. Mixed-gender ministry partnerships that are both personally satisfying and missionally effective are possible, and the attributes represented in this model can help make those partnerships happen. In this concluding chapter, I will begin by detailing four ways that this model might be utilized in a ministry context.

First, this model can lay out a discipleship agenda for individuals and communities. The ten attributes can be used as fodder for any discipleship context, from one-on-one mentoring to small group studies to retreats. I have personally used the model in each of these contexts and have seen individuals and communities take practical and concrete steps toward flourishing in the context of their mixed-gender ministry partnerships.

At one point, I spent several days with a mixed-gender leadership team, walking them through the model. I introduced the model, and then we talked about personal and corporate implications, and the impact was profound. In an evaluation following the training, one leader said, "I gained insight into what roadblocks exist for equality in my ministry partnerships, and some strategies to address them. Importantly, I gained confidence in the theological basis for women in ministry, which helps me to be more hopeful in the way that I work toward flourishing mixed-gender partnerships."[3] Another said, "I learned that I still have some biases and also some pain and hurt regarding this issue that I need to personally work out with God. I realize that I haven't really thought of having these types of conversations in my context. I want to be an advocate not just for myself but also for my female students. I am excited to create trainings and adjust the ways I teach in order to incorporate some of the material." Used as content in the discipleship process, this model can equip individuals and communities to form and maintain flourishing mixed-gender partnerships.

Second, the model can be useful for supervisors or leaders in determining whether or not assigning women and men to work together in ministry would be a wise decision in the first place. One leader I know used the model as a

---

[3]For this person, the theological conviction attribute was particularly useful, but one of the helpful features of the model is its breadth. There are essentially ten different places where individuals and groups can enter into the model. In fact, in one focus group, a respondent observed that the model "touches on all aspects of someone's experience in ministry."

report card of sorts; he picked letter grades for each attribute for both members of the potential partnership and ultimately made the determination that moving forward would not be a good fit at that time. Another supervisor mused that the Together in Ministry model could be a beneficial tool during recruitment and hiring processes.

Third, the model can serve as an evaluative guide in an ongoing mixed-gender ministry partnership. Periodically pausing to compare how a given mixed-gender ministry partnership stacks up in relation to the Together in Ministry model can reveal which aspects are strengths and which are weaknesses. One set of mixed-gender ministry partners who used the model in this way called it a useful "triage tool."

Finally, the content of the model could be useful in a systematized organizational training program. Imagine if a church or organization decided to become proactive in training its members with the material in this book? As a part of a community-wide training curriculum, this model could yield benefits both in the personal satisfaction of the people as well as in the organizational bottom line.

The Together in Ministry model can be used in these four specific ways, but there are doubtless others. My hope is that this content ultimately makes its way into the cultures of our churches and organizations, influencing how we both think and operate in mixed-gender ministry settings.

INTEGRATIVE THEMES

When I present on this model, people often ask me whether there are general themes that weave their way through each of the attributes of the model. In response, I identify two themes: intentionality and courage.

Flourishing mixed-gender ministry partnerships will not just happen. On the contrary, as this book has articulated, many forces conspire to prevent mixed-gender ministry partnerships from flourishing, from theologies that sequester women to the organizational margins, to enshrined ministry philosophies with unintended consequences such as the Billy Graham Rule, to narratives that suggest that mixed-gender friendships are impossible. Overcoming these and other would-be impediments will require individuals and communities to apply focused intentionality.

Intentionality is always required in seasons of change. In his work on adaptive change, Tod Bolsinger notes that "for inspired ideas to take root within the culture of an institution, there must be a series of intentional actions."[4] Each chapter in *Together in Ministry* has concluded with application questions in an effort to help readers take faithful next steps.[5] Pursuing those steps with intentionality can begin the process of greater flourishing in mixed-gender ministry partnerships.[6]

If we are going to see mixed-gender ministry partnerships flourish in our contexts, we will need to be intentional, but we will also need courage. It will take courage to reimagine how we operate in terms of ministry partnerships between women and men. We will need courage to explore new ways of thinking about power. We will need courage to root out and mitigate the subtle yet toxic gender dynamics that adversely affect women. And we will need courage to examine and seek healing in the places of our lives where we experience gender brokenness.

Like intentionality, courage is also required in seasons of change. Indeed, courage is a theme in the change literature. Writing from a faith-based perspective, Alan Roxburgh and Fred Romanuk write, "It takes courage to do the right thing when it is neither easy nor comfortable and to accept the personal consequences of leading people out of familiar habits and patterns toward an alternative future."[7] And writing from a corporate, secular perspective, Bolman and Deal note that leaders "need courage to follow uncharted routes, expecting surprise and pushing ahead when the ultimate destination is dimly foreseeable."[8]

It is courageous intentionality, then, that constitutes the blood that circulates through the body of the Together in Ministry model. As we press into courageous intentionality, we should find greater flourishing in our mixed-gender ministry partnerships.

---

[4]Tod Bolsinger, *Canoeing the Mountains: Christian Leadership in Uncharted Territory* (Downers Grove, IL: InterVarsity Press, 2015), 167.

[5]Credit to Susan Maros for the language of "faithful next steps." Dr. Maros regularly exhorts her students to simply take the faithful next step in applying the things they learn in her classes. Faithful next steps do not have to be revolutionary. In his classic work on change, John Kotter points out the importance of "short-term wins." For Kotter, short-term wins are visible to those engaged in the change process, unambiguous, and clearly related to the change effort. *Leading Change* (Boston: Harvard Business Review Press, 2012), 126.

[6]Tod Bolsinger points out that early interventions should be undertaken "modestly and playfully." As change begins, the goal should be to learn in order to inform the more significant change to come. *Canoeing the Mountains*, 121.

[7]Alan J. Roxburgh and Fred Romanuk, *The Missional Leader: Equipping Your Church to Reach a Changing World* (San Francisco: Jossey-Bass, 2006), 137.

[8]Lee G. Bolman and Terrence E. Deal, *Reframing Organizations: Artistry, Choice, and Leadership*, 4th ed. (San Francisco: John Wiley & Sons, 2008), 436.

FINAL THOUGHTS

When I first started my work on this topic in my doctoral program, I came across a video on YouTube that depicted a woman and man in a climbing gym. For about two minutes, they work together to traverse a course of boulders and climbing features. One moment, the woman pushes the man up to a hard-to-reach handhold, the next moment he is swinging her to a nearby foothold. They are side-by-side and they use one another as leverage; at one point, he carries her from one hold to another. In the end, they are successful in navigating the course, and the video finishes with them both smiling as they exchange a high-five.[9]

When mixed-gender ministry partnerships are truly flourishing, women and men are like these climbers. Working together, sharing leadership, using their respective gifts and strengths, they experience both personal satisfaction as well as missional effectiveness. Not only do the climbers make their goal, they do so with joy. May women and men enjoy a similar experience in the ministry context, and may our mission advance in greater measure as a result.

PROCESSING QUESTIONS

1. At the end of chapter one, you were invited to reflect on which of the ten attributes were strengths and which were weaknesses. Now that you've read through each of the chapters, would you change your answers? If so, how?

2. Thinking of your ministry context, how might you use this model to increase the caliber of the mixed-gender ministry partnerships that you are a part of?

3. What further questions do you have, and where can you go to find answers to your questions?

4. Personally, what are your faithful next steps in contributing to the flourishing of the mixed-gender ministry partnerships in your life and ministry?

5. How are you being led to pray for the mixed-gender ministry partnerships in your context, and who can you invite to pray along with you?

---

[9]See "Partner Climb at Sierra Blair-Coyle's Home Gym," YouTube video, March 5, 2017, www .youtube.com/watch?v=BNWkT21wKCY.

GENERAL INDEX

adverse gender dynamics, 21, 22, 64, 98-110, 118, 151
  Diehl and Dzubinski's examples of unconscious gender bias, 103-5
  mansplaining, 107
  microaggressions, 109
advocacy, 20, 46, 70, 76, 88, 106, 111, 149
appreciative inquiry, 147
Aquila, 68-69, 76
Aquinas, Thomas, 10
Aristotle, 99-100
  See also separate spheres
Barton, Ruth Haley, 27, 37, 54, 57, 123, 133
Becker, Carol, 18, 42
Billy Graham rule, 125-36, 150
Boniface, 88-89, 97
boundaries, 21, 22, 56, 93, 112, 114, 122, 125-36
calling, 40, 42, 57, 71, 80, 81, 85, 105, 130
Calvin, Jean, 11
Chrysostom, John, 10
#ChurchToo, 35, 61, 119, 120, 131
CliftonStrengths assessment, 71
communication, 21, 22, 36, 82, 96, 103, 109, 112, 113-24, 133
  awkwardness in, 36, 59, 98, 108-9, 113-14, 118-19, 121, 123, 133-34
  conflict and, 21, 92, 115, 118, 141
  gender differences in, 82, 120-21
  Jesus and women, 115-17
  listening, 35-38, 50, 81, 96, 107, 122, 137
  See also debrief; question-asking
complementarian theology, 40, 41, 47-49, 51
conflict, 21, 92, 115, 118, 141
courage, 12, 24, 35, 113, 118, 123, 132, 134, 150-51
David, 3, 54-57, 80
debrief, 21, 98, 107-10, 114, 119
discipleship, 6, 31, 43, 53, 59-61, 86, 127, 132, 149
egalitarian theology, 7, 40, 44, 48-51, 140, 144
empathy, 32-33, 35, 38, 80, 82

Enneagram, 57, 71
Euodia, 140-41
ezer, helper, 3-4
fear
  of engaging others' brokenness, 34, 36
  of moral failure, 93, 95-96, 131-32, 135
  of opposite gender, 54
  of theological pushback, 49, 144
flourishing
  definition of, 16-19
  missional effectiveness and, 17-19, 20-21, 23, 32, 61, 64, 67, 72, 86, 106, 114-15, 123, 142, 147, 152
  personal satisfaction and, 17-19, 21, 23, 32-33, 61, 64, 67, 83, 86, 92, 111, 114-15, 123, 142, 147, 149-50
  See also shalom
Franklin, Benjamin, 61
Fuller Theological Seminary, 2
gender bias, 21, 46, 54, 84, 101, 103, 109, 149
  See also adverse gender dynamics
gender brokenness, 20-21, 52-62, 107, 130, 132, 151
gender differences, 20-22, 64, 78-87, 106, 115, 121
  See also communication: gender differences in
gender essentialism, 82-84, 120
gender roles, 81, 84-85
Generation Z (iGen), 95
Genesis vision of gender equality, 2-12, 41, 45-46, 66, 69, 105, 111
giftedness/gifting, 40, 46, 71, 79-81, 85-86, 89, 105, 134, 144, 152
grace, 30, 123
Heath, Chip, and Dan Heath, 145
humility, 30, 51, 53, 57
image of God, 2, 4, 17, 135
intentionality, 1, 12, 21, 24, 33, 58, 60, 61, 64, 70, 93, 98, 106, 113, 118, 123, 132, 134, 137, 139, 141, 150-51

InterVarsity Christian Fellowship, 1, 2, 15, 20, 40, 48-50, 65, 70, 78, 82, 98, 134, 146-48
Jesus, 15, 17, 43, 60
  and the Billy Graham rule, 128-29
  communication, 59, 115-17, 122
  implications of the cross, 7-8, 44
  and a learner's posture, 31-32, 37
  Messianic identity, 6, 31, 116-17, 129
  partnership with women, 5-7, 31, 81
  use of power, 74
Junia, 8, 10, 44
leadership
  bias toward men, 5, 11, 46-47, 54, 84-85, 102, 103-5, 127
  development process, 86, 138
  gender distinctives, 79, 82, 84
  shared models of, 19, 40, 42, 65-65, 69, 71-76, 79, 100-101, 113, 152
  solitary leadership paradigm, 73
  See also gender roles
learner's posture, 20, 29-39, 96
  Jesus and, 31-32
  See also question asking
Lioba, 88-89, 97
listening, 35-38, 50, 81, 96, 107, 122, 137
loneliness, 33, 73, 94
Martha, 6, 81
Mary (from Luke 10), 6, 81
Mary Magdalene, 6, 115-17
mentoring, 37, 48, 60, 86, 104, 149
#MeToo, 35, 61, 119, 120, 131
Mezirow, Jack, 47
mindbugs, 107
misogyny, 5, 8, 10, 11, 43
mixed-gender friendships, 18, 21-22, 34, 88-97, 118-19, 131, 141, 147, 150
  and the apostle Paul, 90-91
  See also siblingship
modeling, 42, 45, 112, 118, 137-46
nature vs. nurture, 79
Paul, the apostle, 43, 68-69, 90-91, 99-101, 139-42
  and egalitarianism, 7, 10, 43-44,
  and female coworkers, 8, 68-69, 90-91, 99-101, 140-41
  public nature of his ministry, 139-42, 144
  and the siblingship paradigm, 95-96
  and the situation in Ephesus, 1, 8-9

personal reflection, 38, 49-50, 67, 70, 74, 108, 121, 144
Phoebe, 8, 44, 90-91, 99-101, 140
pornography, 54, 58
power, 20-22, 45, 65-77, 151
  abuse of, 35, 55, 127
  audit, 75, 77
  definition of, 66
  dynamic in the curse, 4, 70, 127
  releasing power/submission, 30, 70
Priscilla, 44, 68-69, 76
qualitative research, 20, 65
  focus groups, 16, 20, 38, 65, 149
  research interviews, 16, 20, 29-30, 38, 41-42, 53-54, 65, 69-70, 76, 78, 86-87, 89, 101, 109, 113, 137-38, 147
  participant observation, 20, 65, 89, 115
question asking, 30-31, 33-37, 60, 96, 116-17, 120, 122, 134, 145
representation, 21, 82, 95, 137-39, 143, 145
safe spaces to process, 35, 49, 60, 74, 95, 135
separate spheres, 80, 99-100, 119, 140
sex/sexuality, 10-11, 36, 53-54, 58-59, 61, 93, 96, 115, 120, 126-27, 131, 135, 148
shalom, 17, 19
siblingship, 90, 95-96, 119, 134
silence, church's culture of, 36, 59, 71, 95, 119
sponsorship, 70, 86, 101, 104
stained-glass ceiling, 85, 103, 148
stereotypes, 78-81, 86, 105, 121
  See also gender essentialism
Summa Theologica, 10-11
Syntyche, 140-41
Tertullian, 10
theology, 2, 8-9, 11, 40-51, 68, 84, 135, 141-42, 144, 148
  of power, 77
  See also complementarian theology; egalitarian theology
transformative learning theory, 47
trust, 20-21, 32-33, 38, 72, 74, 92, 94, 107, 108, 116-18, 122, 135
violence, gender-based, 35, 119
vulnerability, 30, 35-36
When Harry Met Sally, 93
work/life balance, 21, 93-94

SCRIPTURE INDEX

OLD TESTAMENT

Genesis
1, 2, 69
1:27, 2
1:28, 3, 67
2, 3
2:18, 3
3, 4
3:16, 4
16:1-16, 5
21:9-21, 5

Exodus
15, 5

Numbers
12, 5

Deuteronomy
32:11, 84

Joshua
2, 5

Judges
4–5, 5, 80
4:9, 80

1 Samuel
13:14, 55

2 Samuel
11–12, 55
12:13, 55

13:1-22, 5
15:30, 80

Nehemiah
1:4, 80

Psalms
51, 56, 57
51:6, 56, 132
54, 3
54:3-4, 3
133, 45

Isaiah
66:13, 84

Jeremiah
29:13, 32

Hosea
11:3-4, 84

Micah
6:4, 5

NEW TESTAMENT

Mark
4:1-20, 31
4:10, 31
4:35-41, 132
5:24-34, 6

Luke
10:38-42, 6, 31, 81

John
1:35-42, 116
1:38, 116
4, 31, 59, 117, 129
4:6, 129
4:8, 129
4:26, 117
4:27, 129
10:3-5, 116
11, 81
11:35, 80
20, 7, 117
20:1-18, 115, 117
20:11-18, 6
20:15, 116
20:16, 116
20:17, 117

Acts
8:1, 43
8:3, 43
9:1-19, 43
11:26, 43
16:11-40, 8
17:34, 8
18:2, 68
18:18, 68
18:24-28, 68

Romans
16, 68, 91
16:1, 8, 91
16:1-2, 100
16:2, 91
16:3, 68
16:7, 8, 10

16:12, 8, 91
16:13, 91

1 Corinthians
11:16-33, 139
16:19, 68

Galatians
3, 44
3:26-29, 7, 8
3:28, 7, 10, 44, 140

Philippians
3:17, 140
4:2-3, 140

Colossians
4:15, 8

1 Thessalonians
5:27, 141

1 Timothy
2, 8
2:11-12, 8, 9
2:12, 1

2 Timothy
1:4, 80
1:5, 8
1:15, 140
4:6-8, 139
4:19, 68

Hebrews
11:31, 5

More Titles from
InterVarsity Press and Missio Alliance

Emboldened
978-0-8308-4524-8

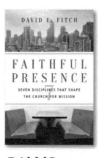

Faithful Presence
978-0-8308-4127-1

Redeeming Sex
978-0-8308-3639-0

**Rediscipling the
White Church**
978-0-8308-4597-2

**Seven Practices for the
Church on Mission**
978-0-8308-4142-4

Sojourner's Truth
978-0-8308-4552-1

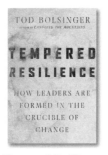

Tempered Resilience
978-0-8308-4164-6

Uncommon Church
978-0-8308-4162-2

White Awake
978-0-8308-4393-0

*For a list of IVP email newsletters, including information
about our latest ebook releases, please visit*
www.ivpress.com/eu1.